Find more of my work at my blog:

www.theauthorstack.com

Find all my work at my website:

www.russellnohelty.com

Bookbub:

https://www.bookbub.com/profile/russell-nohelty

HOW TO BUILD YOUR CREATIVE CAREER

By:
Russell Nohelty

Edited by:
Leah Lederman

Dedicated to every fan who has asked my advice over the last several years, whether through emails, at shows, or at signings. You are the reason I do what I do, and I hope this book gets you further down the path of success.

Paperback ISBN: 978-1-942350-55-2

Second Edition, September 2019

INTRODUCTION

I hate the way creatives treat their livelihoods. There seem to be only two career options for any creative I speak with: a soulless career as a corporate drone or a whimsical flight of fancy pursuing their passions while living in squalor. Go and ask a creative for their business plan, and ninety-nine times out of a hundred you'll be laughed out of the room.

"I'm an artist, not a businessman," they'll say. Break that down for a moment. This person, who is trying to build a list of clients and increase their revenue year over year by *offering products people want to buy,* has flat out stated they are not a business.

That's crazy talk. Creatives are as much a business as a plumber or a web designer or an IT consultant. They have to file taxes, deal with audience building, find clients, negotiate with vendors, and deal with every other nuisance that other businesses encounter; however, they believe themselves cut out from the rest of business like special snowflakes.

It's easy to see why, of course. In creative circles, business is portrayed as soulless, money centric, and dirty. This idea of thinking of art as a business is something that bristles even the most successful creatives. After all, art should never be sullied with money, right?

Wrong.

It's that kind of thinking that devalues artistic endeavors and prevents creatives from making a decent and consistent living. Those who can make a living are in constant competition with people who will do the work "for the exposure," because they've been taught that art is something you pursue above monetary concerns. Therefore, successful artists are consistently underpricing their work relative to their experience to keep up with an undervalued market.

It's the reason that some of the most successful artists of all time died in squalor and misery, their talent only being recognized upon their death. It's the reason companies can exploit creatives for far less than they are worth, making massive profits in the process. Corporations certainly do not hold the same stigma about creating a business from art as creatives do.

In fact, massive industries have built their fortunes on the backs of artists. Marvel, DC—heck, the entire advertising and publishing industries—generate billions upon billions of profits from art every year while creatives can barely make rent.

Well, I am sick of it. I don't blame the companies for exploiting their workers. I blame us, the creatives, and the idea we've lived with for far too long that mixing business and art is gross. It's not that thinking of yourself as a business is a necessary evil; it's not evil at all. Implementing business practices into your art allows you to get better clients, improve your life, and gives you more freedom.

Growing a brand and a business offers you the flexibility to turn down work and have enough money to take vacations with your family; it allows you to save for retirement and prevents you from working your fingers to the bone just to scrape by.

I learned this a long time ago when I was stubborn and ignorant. I thought sales was gross and marketing was evil. I thought people should value my work for its merit alone. I thought people would magically find me…and that puppy dogs cleaned their own poop.

Of course, this isn't the case. The market is flooded with content. It's impossible to stand out from the crowd without a bullhorn. The good news is that it's also never been easier to build an audience and find a market for your work. The tools are already in your hands.

That's what this book is about—how to turn your art into a business and make a career as a creative.

What is a creative? A creative is anybody that makes things. This includes, but isn't limited to: writers, painters, sculptors, craft people, comic book artists, singers, musicians, animators, and people that create things from scratch, with a strong emphasis on people who create products, whether that be books, art prints, jewelry, oven mitts, et al.

I am a writer by trade and a publisher by profession, and my experience skews toward comic books and novels. However, I've done my best to give examples from all creative fields.

I've broken my thoughts into five sections: Creating great content, the basics of selling, building an audience from scratch, making money at live events, and launching a successful product.

Together, these are incredibly powerful tools, but even alone they can make you a better business person. Every lesson is packed with ways to build your career as a creative and start thinking about yourself as a business without feeling yucky inside.

Thank you so much for picking up this book. Just by holding it in your hands, I know you are more serious about your career than 99 percent of creatives I meet. You are ready to make more money as a creative, and you think buying this book is a good idea.

May these pages help you expand your business and give you the freedom you deserve.

PART 1

MAKING GREAT CONTENT

Before we get to selling your art, we have to discuss making great content. It's useless to try to sell something that isn't great.

Why?

Because the world is flooded with great content. There are great artists, writers, sculptors, animators, and every kind of creative you can imagine. You can't walk into a flea market without seeing ten things that will blow you away.

If you're going to compete, you have to make something great and consistently perform at the level of greatness. Once you can make great stuff again and again, then you are in the game.

Wait, did I just say in the game? Do I really mean that making great content doesn't guarantee sales?

Absolutely.

Making great content means you are IN THE GAME. It's the first step to building a career. It doesn't mean you can win the game, or that people will buy from you. It just means that your stuff is now salable on the open market. It means that it's competitive with everything else out there.

Creators often come to me and ask why their stuff isn't selling as well as mine. Sometimes, it's because they stink at sales, but it's usually because their quality sucks. I can immediately tell they took the cheapest route, hired the lowest-priced manufacturer, and still priced their work equivalent to the best available products on the market.

That's crazy. Why would somebody buy their crappy stuff when they can buy something way better for the same price?

Answer: They wouldn't.

You have to outperform—or at the very least *meet*—the market standard before you can expect anybody to consider buying from you.

Sure. They might buy once out of pity. Anybody can be tricked into buying something once, but they won't be lifelong customers. And that's what we are trying to achieve here. We aren't trying to get a one-time customer. We are trying to get a customer for life.

That's what we are going to explore in this section—how we can make great content consistently so we can attract customers who will buy from us forever.

WHAT KIND OF CREATIVE DO YOU WANT TO BE?

The first thing we must do to develop a successful career as a creative is ask ourselves what kind of creative interests we want to pursue. This is called strategic planning. I know it sounds like a stuffy business term, but let me give you an example of why strategic planning is critically important to your career.

When I launched Wannabe Press, I spent the first fourteen months after its inception working inside my business, doing all of the day-to-day work to keep my business afloat. I didn't worry about building for the future. I didn't worry about branding. I didn't worry about my ideal client. All I worried about was the next sale. And that was really unsatisfying. By November of 2015, I was floundering. There was very little growth in my business month after month, and I was going crazy from stress.

That's because I didn't know what was going on in my business. I had no idea what was working in my creative life. I didn't know who was buying my books, or why, I just knew they were being bought. It felt like I learned nothing and was no closer to being successful than the day I launched.

So, what did I do?

I took the month of December 2015 off from my company. That might sound like a luxury, but I was willing to risk one month of sales to figure out what made my business function. I knew I didn't want to flounder in my business, and the only way for it to grow was to discover what I was doing wrong and what I was doing right.

So, I spent the entire month researching what worked and what didn't in my business. I analyzed every show, counted every penny. I read through dozens of papers and analyzed hundreds of other companies trying to glean any secrets I could from them. Once my research was done, I developed several hypotheses about what made successful businesses function. For those of you that slept through high school science like I did, a hypothesis is a possible explanation for a problem that becomes a starting point for further investigation.

By the end of December, I solidified several hypotheses about how to make my company function and developed a plan to make my company more efficient in 2016.

I went back to work in January, implementing and fine tuning plans to test all my hypotheses. The most important of these plans revolved around my company's brand identity. In my market research, I realized most successful companies had a very strong brand identity that was easily recognizable to everybody in the world. I hypothesized that in order to grow exponentially, Wannabe Press needed a similar streamlined identity. I hired a graphic designer to start working on a new mascot and went about rebranding the entire company so people could see one image and immediately know what to expect from us.

By February, we came out of the gate with a redesign that was immediately a massive success. We more than doubled our growth from 2015 to 2016, and our audience exploded. Because of our new mascot, banners, and cohesive brand, people recognized us at show after show, and we were able to continue that conversation online through our improved mailing list and social media presence. More importantly, we were able to target our message to the exact right people instead of shouting into the ether and hoping someone would listen. It's safe to say that real-world testing validated this hypothesis.

Did all of our hypotheses work? No. Some of them crashed and burned. A couple blew up in my face. For instance, I thought there was a market for a membership community specifically targeting creators who wanted to run more effective Kickstarter campaigns. I dropped thousands of dollars on website development and marketing. I spent days creating membership videos. In the end, nobody wanted what I was selling.

That hypothesis ended up being invalidated; however, in testing it I realized there was a hole in the market for teaching people how to build a sustainable creative career. It was a massive success derived from a miserable failure. I never would have been able to find that hole if I didn't start with a hypothesis.

In the same way, you need to start with a hypothesis about what you want out of your career. It doesn't need to be right. It might be wildly inaccurate. It might even blow up in your face; however, in testing your hypothesis, you will learn more about what you truly want out of your career and where your true passions lie. That is the key to successful strategic planning.

How do you start with your own strategic planning? It's as simple as asking a couple of questions:

What creative field do you want to pursue? If you are on the fence, choose one field to start. Remember, we are just building a hypothesis here. You might hate the work you do after testing it, but at least then you'll be able to cross something off your list. When narrowing your focus, crossing something off a list is often as important as finding your ideal career path out of the gate. For the sake of this conversation, I'm going to say that we want to be industrial designers.

What is the ideal company to work for in your chosen field? Even if you want to work freelance and build your own thing, it's important to answer this question because it will give you a company structure and audience to emulate. One of the most important pieces of advice I ever got in business was "Model success." Successful companies spend millions of dollars on marketing. With a little time investment, you can see exactly what works for their business. Those same strategies can work for you, too— with none of the capital investment.

Since we are trying to be industrial designers, our ideal company might be Apple, since they were the pinnacle of design innovation in the first decade of the 2000s.

Who is your favorite creative in your chosen field? This can be any creative you admire, but they need to be in the chosen creative field you want to pursue. They don't have to work for your ideal company, but they shouldn't hate that company either. Then, you can emulate and model the career path they took and use it as a guide.

If we are pursuing the previous thread, then Sir Jonathan Ive, the Chief Design Officer of Apple, could be our favorite creative in the industrial design field. Plotting out his career trajectory can get us close to designing a plan for our own lives.

If you were to pursue this field, where would you want to be in five years? In three years? In one year? In six months? In three months? In one month? In one week? People overestimate what they can achieve in one year and underestimate what they can achieve in five years. Short-term and long-term planning are incredibly important to your success. Short-term planning gives you an immediate goal which is attainable. Long-term planning gives you a vision for the future.

In our Apple scenario, we would need to set a realistic timetable for getting a job with them. Since we are just beginning our journey, a five-year plan to work at Apple is a realistic one.

If you set that as your five-year goal, you can begin to work backward and develop a plan for where you need to be in three years, in one year, and all the way back to what you need to do this very week in order to attain your goal. That might mean enrolling in design school. It might mean watching tutorials on YouTube. It might mean buying a 3D printer. Those little goals will lead you close to your end goal, which is working at Apple.

Now that you have those four questions answered, hang them over your desk, bed, or somewhere else that you can easily see them every day. You should be able to look at your long-term goals and short-term goals constantly and either validate them or invalidate them on the fly.

If your hypotheses were incorrect, that's okay. You can always revise your plan midstream. Don't do it every day though. Make sure to only revise your plan at specific intervals. The first of these intervals should be a short weekly strategy session—plan a time and date every week for revisiting your goals, like Wednesday at 5 p.m. This is an immoveable meeting; so make sure to make it at a time you can commit to every week.

Every quarter, plan a half day (four-hour) strategy session to delve into your goals and make sure you are still on the right path. This session takes an in-depth look at all the data you accumulated about your business in the previous months to readjust your path for the future. It's hard to analyze your overall progress on a week-to-week basis, which is why these quarterly reviews take a more longitudinal analysis of your career.

Every year you should have a daylong session (if not more) to analyze your entire year, invalidate or validate all your previous hypotheses, and create a plan for the year ahead. This is a living, breathing document and if it no longer fits with your goals, then it's okay to change your plan or throw it out and start again.

MAKE IT ONCE. SELL IT FOREVER.

Perhaps the most important concept when it comes to the idea of making great content is that you only have to make the content once, but you have the ability to sell it forever.

This is antithetical to the mindset of most creators, who try to find the cheapest way to make something so they can save a bit of money in the short run, foregoing the prospect of selling it for the next decade.

This is a dangerous mindset. Short-term planning is only part of the equation in building a career. The true value of creating things is in the long-term ability to sell them for the next thousand years.

Take something like *Alice in Wonderland*. Lewis Carroll's famous book was released in 1865. I have read that book multiple times in my life and owned several editions, yet I was born over one hundred years from its release. It's produced so well that it's still printing money for publishers over a century later. That is the power of making the best product you can and then selling it forever.

Another example from the consumer product space would be the Big Mac from McDonald's. The Big Mac was created in 1967 and is still sold to this day with the same "two all-beef patties, special sauce, lettuce, cheese, pickles, onions, on a sesame seed bun."

McDonald's spent millions of dollars testing, researching, and perfecting the Big Mac, and it only costs a couple of bucks to buy.

Why would they do that? Because of long-term planning.

An initial investment of millions led to billions of income in the ensuing decades since its release. They wouldn't have created the Big Mac if they only thought in the short term; they knew investing in a great product could pay off forever.

That should be the philosophy we take with our own content. Creators who cheap out on book covers, or paper stock for their prints, or website design, or hiring artists will always have trouble selling their content compared to those who don't, and in the end they will not have saved much money.

Let me give you an example with some hard numbers.

The difference in paying an artist $50 and $100 a page in the short term is the difference of a few thousand dollars. For the rest of this example, let's call the $50/page artist "Frank" and the $100/page artist "Jill."

On a 100-page book, Frank will cost you $5,000. Meanwhile, Jill will cost you $10,000. Up front, that seems like a huge difference, and, initially, it is. But that additional initial investment pays dividends over time.

You see, using Jill means hiring a more experienced artist who will help you sell books. A lot more books. Especially with comics, art is what drives sales. People come for the art and stay for the story. Conservatively, an experienced artist can increase book sales by ten times, but it's usually much more than that. So, if Frank's art can sell one hundred books for you in a year, then Jill's art can sell one thousand books in a year.

On a $10 book, Frank's art would sell $1,000 of revenue in one year. In the same time frame, Jill's art would sell $10,000 in revenue. Which means after one year on the market, Jill has paid for herself while Frank still needs to recoup $4,000 to make your investment worthwhile.

That's a dramatic difference, but on a longer-term horizon there is an even more dramatic difference...

If we plot these two books out for ten years, Jill has returned $100,000 on ten thousand sales while Frank has only returned $10,000 on one thousand sales.

Yes, they both have earned out, but Jill cost you $1 per unit sold ($10,000 initial investment/10,000 units sold) while Frank cost you $5 per book sold ($5,000 initial investment/1,000 units sold).

Isn't that incredible?

The more expensive artist is actually five times cheaper in the long term than the less expensive one, which is something Marvel learned decades ago.

Now, I'm not saying every artist is worth their price, or that you can expect to get ten times more from every book you do—and you should certainly price compare everything—but I will say that the difference in sales is astounding when you invest in your product up front.

You see it with prints, blog posts, and sculptures too. If you spend a little bit of time and effort investing in your product on the front end, your payoff can be dramatic.

FINISH THINGS

When people ask me how I got to the place I am today, I tell them that it's because I finished things. I finished novels. I finished graphic novels. I finished comic books. I finished podcasts. I finished nearly everything I set my mind out to do.

Even when I didn't like something, I still finished it. Why? Because it is in the *finishing* of something that learning happens. It's not in the starting something. This is because it's very easy to take something to 90 percent completion. You can begin a novel today and have it finished in a couple of weeks if you are only concerned about a first draft.

However, in writing, the true mastery is in the editing. It's in discovering how everything fits together to make a cohesive story. Those synapses in your brain only fire once you have completed the first draft and started synthesizing all that gooey information into something that makes sense.

There's a very good reason for this. Generally, the first draft of anything is garbage, whether it's the sketches for a new piece of artwork or the first pass of this book.

This book truly was rubbish on my first pass. The sentences didn't make sense, the flow wasn't right, and whole chapters needed to be reworked from scratch. The only positive thing I could say about this book after the first draft was that at least it was on the page. It wasn't publishable, but it was out of my head. Once it was on paper, I could mold it like a hunk of clay.

Let's examine that clay metaphor more closely for a moment. Have you ever played with clay? It's really hard to work with, at least for me. I'm so jealous when I watch masters take a piece of clay and effortlessly turn it into a beautiful piece of art.

At least, the clay ends up beautiful. In the beginning, though, it looks exactly like every other piece of clay. Even halfway through working, their sculpture looks like something I could do. Most of the time, their work looks like a hot mess even as it nears completion. Then, in one singular moment, the mastery kicks in and they make it something perfect that I could never accomplish in my wildest dreams.

That's what I mean by finishing things. You don't learn much from getting the sculpture halfway done. Anybody can do that. It's not hard to create a sculpture form that looks vaguely okay and give up. It's not hard to draw a sketch, or doodle in a sketch book. Most people are capable of that much. Real skills come into to play when developing that raw form into a finished product.

And your first finished product is going to be awful. Just face it now. But you will learn so much about technique that your next finished product will be better. With each successive finished project, you will only get better, and faster as well. While it might take you ten hours to finish a crappy art print today, next year—after finishing dozens of them—you might be able to crank out a masterpiece in only a couple of hours.

Each time you finish a project, you strengthen the connective tissue in your brain that helps you figure out the whys and hows of the craft; you learn what works and what doesn't…and that's when you start leveling up quickly.

As you continue to complete projects, not only does your skill level increase, but your reputation in the creative community grows. The more projects you finish, the more professional you will become. The mark of an amateur is only starting things. The mark of a professional is finishing them. By completing a project, you are seen as somebody who finishes things, and that is a rare quality. In finishing things, you start believing in yourself more as well.

EVERYBODY SUCKS AT FIRST AND THAT'S OKAY

Ira Glass is one of my all-time favorite creatives. He's been the producer and host of *This American Life* since 1995. *This American Life* is one of the seminal shows on American radio. It might be THE seminal radio show.

But he's not one of my favorite creatives because of *This American Life*. He's one of my favorites because he's responsible for my favorite quote of all time. I thought about butchering it through paraphrase, but instead I will provide it here in its entirety, even though it's long. It's just that awesome.

Nobody tells this to people who are beginners, I wish someone told me. All of us who do creative work, we get into it because we have good taste. But there is this gap. For the first couple years you make stuff, it's just not that good. It's trying to be good, it has potential, but it's not. But your taste, the thing that got you into the game, is still killer. And your taste is why your work disappoints you. A lot of people never get past this phase, they quit. Most people I know who do interesting, creative work went through years of this. We know our work doesn't have this special thing that we want it to have. We all go through this. And if you are just starting out or you are still in this phase, you gotta know it's normal and the most important thing you can do is do a lot of work. Put yourself on a deadline so that every week you will finish one story. It is only by going through a volume of work that you will close that gap, and your work will be as good as your ambitions. And I took longer to figure out how to do this than anyone

I've ever met. It's gonna take a while. It's normal to take a while. You've just gotta fight your way through.

This quote was pulled from a 2009 interview Ira Glass did with Public Radio International, but it became famous when creatives started taking the original audio and making incredible videos with it. I highly recommend you type in "Taste Gap + Ira Glass" into YouTube and listen to it for yourself about a hundred times.

This quote is a very Ira Glass way of saying you suck when you start out, but you shouldn't let it stop you. The sucking is what stops lots of talented artists from continuing on to greatness. Most people will try something for a while, get bummed out that their work is crappy, and just give up. What they put on the page just isn't what they see in their mind's eye.

I have a secret for you.

Nobody can get on the page exactly what they envision in their mind's eye. I've talked to thousands of creatives and every one of them had trouble putting exactly what was in their mind into the finished product. All they could ever do was get as close as possible to what they envisioned and hope it was good enough. That's all you can ever do as well.

The flat out honest truth is that you aren't very good when you begin. And that's okay. Nobody is very good when they start out. Stephen King, Picasso, and Beethoven sucked when they first sat down to fulfill their greatness. Some people advance more quickly than others, but we all start out sucking. It's only through practice and determination that we become great.

It's important not to compare yourself to other artists who are further ahead on their journey than you. You don't see the thousands of hours it took them to master their craft. All you see is the end result.

If you want to feel better about your own art, google your favorite artist and check out some of their first work. I'm not talking about first published work. I'm talking about the first work they ever posted online. Most of them forget about the first art they posted and never take it down. There are also whole threads on Twitter and Reddit where artists show their first works and how they've improved.

It's startling how crappy your favorite artist was even a few years before they broke into the mainstream.

They sucked too, just like everybody does at first; the difference is they didn't let that stop them. They kept going. They completed projects. They finished things. They learned. They improved. And then they broke through. In that order.

DON'T MAKE YOUR DREAM PROJECT FIRST

Almost everybody has their ideal project, something they've been dreaming of since they were children; something that will set the world on fire. Whenever I meet somebody with a project like that, and they are at the beginning of their career, I tell them the same thing: Wait.

Don't do that dream project first. Wait until you are ready. Fail on smaller projects you don't care about, where it doesn't matter. Fail where you don't have a massive emotional stake in what you are making. Don't fail on the project that sets your soul on fire.

Why?

Well, there are a couple reasons.

1. **You aren't skilled enough yet.** You have a long way to go before you can make something amazing, and until you can make something amazing, it's useless—maybe even harmful—to try to make your dream project. Making smaller projects will help you hone your craft until you are ready for your massive epic.

2. **You don't have the cash.** Because you are at the beginning of your career, you don't have the money necessary to make your dream project with your dream team. Instead, you should be making small projects you can fund, and over time you will be able to fund bigger and bigger projects. Eventually, you will be able to mount that dream project.

3. **You don't have the clout.** Usually, dream projects involve massive scale and scope, something that requires people to buy into your dream. Because you don't have a track record, you can't convince anybody of import to do anything with you. Instead, focus on building up your career so people will want to work with you. Build your career through smaller projects and finishing things.

A great example of a person who didn't pursue their dream project first is my friend David Lawson, Jr. Dave and I met years ago, when I was the director of photography for a short film he was producing, *Silent Lucidity*. This wasn't a big project. It was all set in one room and dealt with a guy slowly going insane as he tried to break the world record for sleep deprivation. It was a small project. I think we shot it over one weekend. But he finished it.

Then, Dave and I lost touch for a few years. When we finally reconnected in LA, I saw he had developed a name for himself and completed incrementally bigger and bigger projects until he was able to fund the kinds of projects he wanted to make. The point is, he didn't go for that dream project first. He made a solid project he could fund and then kept getting bigger opportunities as he proved himself.

This is the ideal way to build a career, through incrementally bigger projects. That's not how most creatives want to work, though. More often than not, they end up abandoning careers because they can't get their dream project created right out of the gate. The project always suffers, or completely fizzles out, from a lack of one or more of the above factors. They spend so much time, energy, and effort on creating one project that even if they finish it, they burn out.

Meanwhile, other people are creating, failing, iterating, and improving. They are able to finish project after project and get better with each piece they put into the world. Then, once their skills match their ambitions, they're able to pursue their dream project not just with zeal and passion, but with the skills required to make it amazing.

This is not me saying don't ever work on your dream project. It's me saying that you should build up to it. Just like buying a starter home is not the end goal of home ownership, your first project isn't the end goal of a creative career. You need to build up cash deposits and momentum to buy that dream home.

It's the same with your dream project.

THE SECRET TO BEING LUCKY

You won't get your big break before your time. This is an unfortunate truth of being a creative. It doesn't matter who you know—until you are good enough to create mind-blowing content, nobody is going to hire you.

So many creatives believe that meeting Stan Lee or Steven Spielberg will change their lives. The thing is that it just might. It might change your life, but not until you are ready for it. If you meet Steven Spielberg and hand him your piece of garbage short film, he's not going to care.

If you meet Steven Spielberg with your earth-shattering movie, he might take notice. He might not, but he might if you catch him on just the right day. But that chance meeting is luck. You have no control over luck. What you have control over is your preparation.

If you prepare properly, opportunities will present themselves. If you put yourself in the right situations, opportunities will happen. If you are prepared, then you will be able to make the most of those opportunities. The right opportunities can take years to cultivate, like pulling on a rubber band. As you pull back, the tension grows and grows. The harder you pull on the band, the more force it has when you finally release it.

The trick is to find these opportunities before you are prepared to utilize them and cultivate contacts until they will happily help to advance your career. This is possible even if you are at the beginning of your career and haven't created anything of import yet.

 So, how do we do that?

There's an old saying among creatives: "Good, nice, and on time. You need two in order to succeed." Being good means you have the talent required to do the job. Being nice means people think you are generally pleasant and affable. Being on time means you deliver on or before a deadline.

As the saying goes, you need two in order to succeed. If you are nice and on time, you don't have to be that good. If you are good and nice, you don't have to be on time. If you are good and on time, you don't have to be that nice. It follows that if you want to find opportunities, you have to master two of those qualities.

At the beginning of your career, you aren't very good—at least not compared to where you will be in the future (with hard work and dedication, and finished projects). The only two things you have control over are being nice and on time. If you can master those two, opportunities will present themselves if you put yourself in the right situations.

If you can just be nice and on time at first, even if you suck at your chosen profession, people will want to be around you. Over the years, you will build a massive rolodex of influential people who want to work with you. Eventually, with enough practice, you will learn to be really good at your job, too.

Possessing all three of these skills is what I call the holy trinity of success, and it's critical to build your career. I've found it over and over in the top performers of every creative field. If you can start out just being on time and nice, people will want to help you. If you keep working at your craft, you will eventually get good. If you can be good, nice, and on time, there will be no stopping you.

It's important to note that when you get your opportunities by being nice and on time, these will be lower-end opportunities. They won't be hiring you into your dream career; they will be using you for grunt work.

If you can do that work with a smile, you will build up enough trust with people that they will assuredly want to help you at the opportune moment—but don't ask for that help until you are ready. When you can create great content, it will be a no brainer for them to work with you.

DEALING WITH CRITICISM

Whenever somebody creates, there are always critics. Most of those critics will be people you don't know, and that's hard enough. Some of those critics may be your family or even your friends. It's incredibly difficult to continue in the face of intense criticism, especially from people you love.

In fact, even to this day I take criticism a hundred times harder than I do praise. Nice things roll off my back; but no matter how many people praise my work, if even one person criticizes it, my entire day is ruined.

And that's massive improvement!

It used to be that my entire month was ruined. Then, I cut it down to my entire week. Eventually, I got that down to a single day.

I've gotten exceedingly good at dealing with criticism, but it took a lot of work. There are several tricks I learned in my career to allow me to keep going even in the face of extreme criticism and negativity.

1. **Surround yourself with positivity.** The first step in being able to survive criticism is to surround yourself with other people who are as crazy as you, who believe in you, and who are working toward the same goal as you. For work to be good it can't be for everybody. Work without a point of view doesn't resonate, and if you have a point of view then some people won't agree with it. That's natural, but if you want the energy to keep going, then it's incredibly important to have some people who believe in your point of view.

2. **Cut out negative people.** You will eventually have to cut at least one negative person out of your life. It's never easy and it's always sad, but it's better to cut out a critical person than let them drag you down into the muck with them. One unrelentingly critical person can derail you creatively for months, years, or even a lifetime.

This doesn't mean to cut out people because they raise valid and helpful criticisms. Those people are angels. You need to hold those people close and never let go. \

I'm talking about negative people who criticize out of spite. There is a big difference between somebody giving constructive criticism to make you better and somebody who is negative just to drag you down.

It's not your job to keep negative people in your life. It's not your job to cater to their whims. It's not your job to make them feel better. It's not your job to be their punching bag. It's not your job to let them derail you.

It's your job to be the best person you can be, pursue your career with abandon, and put yourself in the best position to win.

3. **Don't rely on others for validation.** Part of why we create is so other people can experience what we do and, on some level, love it. There is a difference between wanting other people to experience your work and needing them to like it in order to validate your creation. Relying on other people for validation means that if they don't like it, you won't do it. This viewpoint has stopped thousands of talented artists. If you are able to validate yourself,

criticism will sting and rejection will still hurt, but you will be able to move on from it.

4. **Understand that showing your work brings more positive than negative.** Many artists refuse to show their work to anybody for fear of criticism, but the positives of showing work far outweigh the negatives. Even if your work gets a universally bad reaction, asking the right questions allows you to understand why it was reviled so that you can improve for next time. That's never the case, though. Everybody won't hate what you do. You will always be able to find some people who like your work, and that's what gives you the strength to carry on. Each time you release a piece, more and more of those people will find your work, and you will be able to build a following. The more positive reinforcement you receive, the more likely you are to continue.

5. **Just because one person didn't like your work doesn't mean everybody won't like it.** One person is only one person in a world of seven billion people. For every person who dislikes your work, there's another one who loves it. If you focus your efforts on finding those people who love it and away from people that don't, you will be better able to survive criticism.

6. **It's usually not personal.** Just because people don't like your work doesn't mean they don't like you. I have plenty of friends who don't get my work, don't buy my work, and don't care about my work. That's okay. Those people can still love me without financially supporting me, just like I love them without supporting their work as an accountant or

lawyer or whatever they do. Sometimes, it is personal, and those people need to be taken out of your life, but usually criticism or lack of interest has nothing to do with you as a person.

The fact is, it's always hard to deal with criticism, no matter your age or success level. These tricks have worked for me only because I was willing to get out into the world and try things. In the end, I also know that I would rather have a critical reaction than an indifferent one, because at least they had a reaction. If I evoked a negative emotion in somebody, there's a good chance I can evoke a positive one in somebody else.

That's the most important part of dealing with criticism. You need to get out into the world and show your work to people, because it's in the showing that you build a thick skin and develop the resilience to carry on.

WHAT ARE YOU TRYING TO SAY?

Point of view is more important than talent. I've seen the most technically proficient artwork in the world do nothing for audiences, while a simple mixed media piece has brought them to tears…all due to its point of view.

Point of view is why you can tell Frank Miller's work from Skottie Young's, and Mike Mignola's from Rob Liefeld's. You might not like all of those artists, but you can tell their work apart from the moment they put pen to paper. More importantly, their fans flock to their work because it speaks clearly to them.

To make great content, you need a strong point of view. You need a slant on the world. You need something that separates you from the rest of the creatives on the planet.

Let's do a thought experiment. Think about Tim Burton for a moment. Now think of the kinds of projects that would be perfect for Tim Burton's view of the world. Can you imagine a couple?

Of course you can. His distinct style has been developed in the public zeitgeist for decades.

That clarity of vision makes a good point of view. Tim Burton won't be a good fit for 99.9 percent of movies, but point of view is not about that. Your goal is not to be on everybody's list of candidates, it's to be the number one candidate for the right person. Those projects you just imagined for Tim Burton, could you imagine anybody else directing them and doing as good a job? Probably not.

That is the power of a strong point of view. With a solid point of view, you don't have to pitch yourself. Your ideal audience comes to you.

Point of view is the hardest part to nail down in a creative life, however. It takes life experience and practice to figure out. It's why you need to make a lot of different things and finish all of them. Once you've completed a body of work, you can look back, think about your point of view, and figure out what it is you are trying to say.

If you don't have a point of view, it's a bit like making plain white socks. Nobody hates plain white socks and we all buy them, but we don't care about what brand we buy. Most of us buy whatever's cheapest. Every time we buy, we buy a different brand—whatever's on sale—because we just don't care about plain white socks. You don't want to be plain white socks.

On the other hand, a point of view is like having the brightest, pinkest, dragoniest socks on the planet. They won't be everybody's cup of tea, but those who love bright pink dragon socks will flip their lid and buy ten pairs. They'll look through the designer's collection and buy up all of their stuff. They'll sign up to receive updates for when the new dragon socks come out. Nobody has ever signed up to find out when the next pair of plain white socks launches.

That's the power of a point of view.

Don't worry if you don't have a point of view yet. That's normal when you first start out. The more you create, the more connective thread you will find between your work, and the stronger your point of view will become. One of the reasons artists become more successful later in their career is because they've developed a strong point of view.

If you have already created a decent body of work, it's time to look back on it and ask yourself, what am I trying to say here?

INTERNAL VS. EXTERNAL MOTIVATION

When it comes to living a creative life, there are two types of motivation you can use to find meaning in your work. These forces can drive you toward success or madness, depending on which one you choose.

The first is external motivation. There are many types of external motivation—the desire for fame, glory, money, or some sort of validation outside of yourself which will make your work meaningful.

Most people I encounter begin their creative life focused on these external motivations. They want to be actors because of a desire to walk the red carpet and make lots of money; they want to paint so they can be displayed in the Met or the Louvre; they want to work for Marvel because millions of people will see their work and recognize them.

People motivated by external factors, however, quickly fade out. Let's face it: Most artists will never be on exhibit at a prestigious gallery, or work for Marvel, or achieve any sort of fame. This realization hits people like a ton of bricks, and they run away without ever looking back.

There is a powerful YouTube compilation where celebrities like Lady Gaga, Russell Brand, and Eric Clapton talk about the subject of external motivation. It's called "Celebrities Speak Out on Fame and Materialism" by Think for Yourself. It's a harrowing video to watch, as dozens of celebrities discuss how relying on external motivations to validate your life is a hollow pursuit. The only true way to succeed and be fulfilled is to be internally motivated by the love of creating something. This is the second type of motivation, internal motivation.

Being internally motivated means your validation comes from the satisfaction of creating something, not from somebody appreciating it. It means you can motivate yourself instead of relying on other people to motivate you. It's a bonus when others appreciate your work, but the true validation comes from making it in the first place.

Additionally, internal motivations create better art, because you are not hamstrung by what society wants you to create. With external motivation, you are creating for other people; with internal motivation, you are creating for yourself. You are not looking for the right thing to make so people will like you. You are making something that is unique to you. Incidentally, by making something unique to you it becomes easier to find an audience for your work.

I'm not saying that external validation isn't wonderful. There's nothing like selling something you've made; however, the sale of the product should be a bonus on top of the creation of something great.

I'm also not saying you should create without ever worrying about something's salability. This is a book about making a career as a creative after all, not about creating unsalable material. The first step in creating great content is to actually make stuff for the sake of making it.

At the beginning of your creative pursuits, little of what you make is going to be salable. Until you can hit that stride of making consistently great work, it's important to create for the sake of creating and let that be its own reward.

Then, when you get to the level where you can create salable material, you can hold true to that internal motivation as a rudder while you look for ways to sell your work to a mass audience.

A perfect example of this is Laika. They are a stop motion animation house in a world full of computer-generated animation. Yet they have still been able to find an audience and put out *Coraline*, *The Box Trolls*, *ParaNorman*, and *Kubo and the Two Strings*. Their work is commercially successful even though most animation houses moved away from stop motion years ago.

Any company motivated solely by external motivations would have moved into the world of computer animation along with everybody else, but Laika is motivated by something different. Their main motivator is a love of stop motion animation and their desire to work in that medium. They are internally motivated, and that has allowed them to build an audience that believes in their vision.

By developing that internal motivation, you will never be devastated when a product doesn't catch on, because the true value was in the creation of it. When you are able to rely on yourself for validation, you can always keep going even in the face of tremendous adversity.

YOU WILL NEVER BE THE BEST

There is an unfortunate truth you must come to terms with when you create stuff: You will never be the best in the world.

There will always be somebody further ahead than you. There will always be somebody with a bigger audience, doing bigger things, making more money, and getting better gigs than you.

And that's okay.

The great thing about being a creative today is you don't have to be the best in the world. In fact, even the concept that there can be an objective "best" is antiquated. There is no best. There are only people trying to carve out their own little place in the world.

When you look at the world of comics, who is the best writer? I could make the case for Matt Fraction, Geoff Johns, Mark Waid, Brian K. Vaughn, Brian Michael Bendis, Scott Snyder, and a dozen others. All of them could be the best writer in the world…but none of them really are.

What they all have are different audiences of different sizes and tastes. They all have people who love their stuff and people who hate their stuff.

Not one of them is decidedly the best.

They are all part of a creative melting pot, doing different cool things. If an editor or fan wants a Mark Millar story, they know where to find his work. If they want a Frank Miller story, they can find that too.

However, none of those writers are the best, and you won't be either.

This idea of being the best in the world is toxic to a creative career anyway. It puts you in competition with the peers you should be building friendships with, and it takes you away from the important task of being the best creative you can be for yourself and for your fans.

That's a never-ending pursuit. You can never stop trying to be the best you can be, because that target changes over time. The best you can be today will be much different than the best you could be in three years, and in ten years after that.

So, don't worry about being the best in the world. Just worry about being the best you can be. If you have to be in competition with somebody, compete to be better than who you were yesterday.

IT TAKES A LONG TIME TO BE GREAT

Nobody gets where they want to be overnight. All of the overnight successes I have ever known are the result of roughly ten years of hard, grueling work. They may look lucky from the outside, but that luck is predicated on a decade of grinding in the trenches. It's work that happened behind the scenes before they ever broke out as a success.

My friend Scout Raskin, a successful animation producer, received an early acting success by being cast in *Cry Baby* starring Johnnie Depp and directed by John Waters. She was the talk of my elementary school. She was the golden child; the kid who made good.

That should have been her big break, right?

Wrong.

After graduating college, she moved out to LA and spent the next decade struggling to make it as an actor, writer, and producer.

She invested tens of thousands of dollars of her own money making animated shorts. She took job after job as an accountant, then as a budget specialist, all the while producing content for herself and others. She finally landed a position producing jobs on small shows, which led to bigger shows, which led to some of the most popular animated shows on the planet.

If you look at Scout now, it's easy to say she blew up overnight, but for somebody who's known her since elementary school, I can tell you she never had it easy. She's worked doggedly for every break. You might say she's a twenty-year overnight success. That's the kind of dedication every overnight success story has behind it.

I have good news and bad news for you. The bad news is there is no shortcut to greatness. It takes time, effort, and energy.

The good news is life is long. You will be alive for 25,000 days, give or take. While ten years may seem like forever, a decade is only around 15 percent of your life. If you start chugging along now, you can create consistently great content with decades left to work on it at the top of your game.

If you don't start today, though, you are wasting your time. While it's true that life is long, every day you delay is another day you aren't working toward reaching your goals. There's no reason to delay your passions even one more moment, because success is more than possible.

I have a mantra: 1,000 words a day is 365,000 words a year.

Those thousand words take me about an hour a day to complete. Day by day those thousand words don't mean much, but at the end of the year it's a mountain of work. That mountain of work formed the foundation of my creative career.

The same is true with your own career. If you can create a mountain of work and refine it into salable pieces, you'll be able to create great content consistently and effectively for the rest of your life. Then, it's all about taking those pieces and selling them, which is what we're going to talk about next.

PART 2

THE BASICS OF SELLING

Before we can get into the nitty gritty of building a career, it's important to discuss the basics of salesmanship. I used to fight with creatives tooth and nail over the value of learning sales and marketing.

Eventually, I learned better.

I told them that if they are happy with the level of their career and didn't want to improve their prospects, then they could get away without ever learning sales or marketing. Even if they were unhappy with their career, they didn't have to listen to a word I said, as long as they didn't complain about it. Because that's the sticky wicket: You can't complain if you don't try to change.

If they were unhappy with their career and ready to change, though, that was a different story. If they wanted to make more money and increase their audience, then I could supercharge their creative life.

This is the same offer I make to you, dear reader:

If you are not ready to take sales and marketing seriously, then this is not the book for you.

If you believe selling your products is a yucky proposition, then I am not the right person to guide you.

If you rail against the prospect of marketing, then please put this book down. It's not for you. Not yet.

However, if you are ready to make a career out of your creative pursuits, then it's time to dive down the rabbit hole and build the foundational elements you need to make a business out of your artistic life.

Ready? Then let's dive in.

WHY SHOULD PEOPLE BUY FROM YOU?

Creatives are under the dangerous assumption that if they create great content people will find and buy their stuff simply because it's awesome. That's just not true.

The truth is that making great content does nothing but put you in the game and make it feasible for people to buy your work. It doesn't guarantee sales. It doesn't guarantee anything. After all, everybody has great content. You can't hope to be successful as a creative if you don't create great content.

It would be like a company saying they created a car that didn't explode. That's not special. That doesn't win over any fans. That's what you expect from a car. In the same way, people expect great content when you are a creative. The act of making it puts you on par with Stephen King and every other amazing artist in the world.

Now that you can make great content, the real question is why would somebody buy from you instead of the thousands of other people who make equally amazing content? Why would they buy your book over another, more established writer? Why would they hang your painting on a wall instead of a more renowned artist? Why would they hire you to build their logo when they could hire a more well- known firm?

People aren't going to buy from you just because you're awesome. Well, at least it's not *only* because you are awesome. It's because of two factors: The **Value**

Proposition of what you have to offer and the **Unique Selling Point** that sets you apart.

The **Value Proposition** is the tangible result somebody will get from buying your product. When you are selling a solution, this can be something like "lose sixty pounds in twenty days," or "build your retirement funds from zero to a million dollars in the next year." These are value propositions which are easy and tangible to understand. If you buy that product, you will see measurable change in your life.

With a creative product, value is harder to determine. It deals much more with the emotional attachment a buyer has to your product than with its tangible benefit. The value they might see is meeting an artist in person and having them sign their work, the subject matter of your work might resonate with them, or it might be the fact they are getting a handmade, completely original piece of art. These are all ways to emotionally resonate with your client, and every client will resonate with different products for different reasons.

However, there are tangible value propositions you can offer with creative products, too. For instance, cutting the cost of your product by 25 percent makes people believe they are getting a better deal. Additionally, offering a 2-for-1 discount is another way to give tangible value to a product. Even if you plan on selling a product for three dollars, it is better to price it at five dollars so you can discount it down to three. People see the value in something as originally priced and are always after a deal.

JCPenney used this strategy for years. They priced their product higher than their intended selling price so they could mark it down and show people they were getting a value. They changed this policy for a short while and made their pricing more transparent. Customers hated this change and sales plummeted, because in the buyer's mind they weren't getting as good a deal as before. It was a disaster for JCPenney, but it shows how powerful the idea of a discount really is and how a company can misalign themselves with the value proposition of their customers.

When deciding on your value proposition, it's important to understand not all buyers will resonate with your value proposition. That's okay. Your job is not to attract all buyers. It's to attract the right ones for your offer.

Because of this, it's critically important to ask yourself what the value proposition is that you are offering to your potential clients. Is your value based on the lowest price, the best customer service, the highest quality, or on some other factor?

If you can narrow this down, it will help define your pitch to potential clients and justify the price you charge. Additionally, it will help determine where you stand in the market and how much your product should cost to make.

A **Unique Selling Point** is simply what makes your product one of a kind. The unique selling point sets you apart from every other creative on the planet. It's something only you have.

When somebody comes to your store, they have the choice of thousands, if not millions, of creatives. Your job is to figure out how you are different and why somebody should buy from you. It's not the buyer's job to decide to buy from you; it's your job to convince the buyer you are the right fit for them.

Your unique selling point might be that you print all your artwork in a certain way, or that you use certain materials.

It might have to do with your world view, the types of products you make, or the subject matter of your artwork. The unique selling point is something nobody else has except for you.

My friend Leen Isabel makes a comic book about pole dancing. While the book is great, the unique selling point is that it's the only comic book I've ever seen about pole dancing that is made for female pole dancers instead of oversexualized boys. That unique hook resonates with her intended audience. *Pole Dancing Adventure* isn't for everybody, but its unique selling point makes the right person immediately attracted to her book.

If you can determine the value proposition and unique selling point in your work, you will be on the path toward figuring out everything else related to your business. It will give you a direction for your branding, your ideal customer, and everything else that we talk about for the rest of this book.

So, what is your value proposition? Where do you stand in the market? Are you more concerned with quality or quantity of sales? What do you want to convey to your customers about the value of your product? What separates you from the rest of your competition? Why are you unique?

If you can answer those questions, you will be well on your way to building your career. If you can't, then this is the time to start thinking about it! Jot down some notes and ask a trusted friend or critic.

ARE YOU A GOOD PERSON?

I want to show you a mindset shift that can change your entire opinion about sales and marketing. It's like a psychological parlor trick.

Ready?

Let's do it then. First, I have to ask you a question. Do you consider yourself a good person?

Don't respond with some flippant answer, either. Really think about it in the recesses of your soul. Do you think you are a good person? Would you help your loved ones if they were in a jam? Would you come to the aid of somebody in need if you could? Do puppies and kitties give your tummy flutters?

Seriously, do you think you are a good person?

I'll bet you do.

Most people, in the dark depths of their mind, believe themselves "good." It's part of the human condition to justify our own actions to make us seem like the good guys. I've asked hundreds of people that same question and every single one of them has said yes to it.

I'm going to assume you said yes to the first question, too. Since we can agree you are a good person, I have one more question for you.

Do you think your art can change lives for the better?

I don't mean your creativity will change the world. I don't mean somebody is going to come up tomorrow and tell you that you saved them in a profound way. I don't mean your work is going to cause a life-altering shift in somebody's personality.

I'm simply asking, do you think your work can help edify somebody's soul and make them a more complete human being? Do you think that by reading your book or buying your painting or looking at your art, a person can become happier, better, or more enlightened—for even one moment?

Of course you do. Every creative does.

Every person I've asked this question has answered yes without a second thought. I don't think there is a creative person alive who doesn't think their art can affect people. After all, art is a communal experience. Art is about baring your soul and hoping other people see themselves reflected back in what you've done.

So, if we can agree that you are a good person and your work can affect people's lives in a positive way, then you have a moral imperative to tell as many people about your art as possible, because as a good person, you want to change as many people's lives for the better as possible.

This is not an option. It is a duty to make people's lives better. Who knows what will happen if you show your work to the right person. They might just have a transformative experience. They might have been holed up in a shell, thinking nobody understood them, and then you showed up and changed their world. I know this can happen because it's happened to me.

You don't know what could happen, but as a good person you are morally bound to tell everyone you can about your work if you believe it will change lives. Is that a bit corny? Yeah it is, but it's equally true and meaningful. It's the mindset shift that changed my entire life.

Sales and marketing isn't about being a car salesman. It's about showing people what you can do to help them, and hoping they want to be helped by what you have to offer. If they don't want your help, then that's the cost of doing business and you move on to the next person.

However, if they do want your help, then you might have just changed somebody's life, opened their eyes to a whole new way of thinking, and done your good deed for the day...all while making a little bit of money, as well.

THE SALES FUNNEL

When creatives delve into sales for the first time, they often complain their daily work doesn't pay off quickly enough. They call people, email prospects, and have meetings with potential customers, but when they don't get any new clients in the first few weeks of starting their business, it makes them want to abandon it altogether.

Of course, that's a mistake. There is a simple reason why their hard work isn't paying off immediately. Selling is all about delayed gratification. In sales, we build for the future, not the present. Very few customers will ever close on a deal the day you meet them. Customers need time to get to know you, like you, and build trust with you before they buy your product or service. What you do today is predictive of your success in six to eight weeks.

That's right.

Your hard work today won't pay off for nearly two months. This is what hampers many artists from growing their business. They give up before they could ever realistically succeed. We live in a world of instant gratification, and success in business is a long-term payoff. Over time, your hard work compounds through the success of your sales funnel.

A sales funnel is no different than a funnel you would use in your kitchen or to put oil into your car—wide at the top with a narrow bottom. Into the top of the funnel goes potential customers and out the bottom comes clients. It's as simple as that.
There are four stages in my sales funnel. The first stage is that **people need to know you exist**. This means you need

a strong internet presence, a killer in-person networking strategy, and a dynamite brand.

At this stage of the funnel, you aren't trying to find the right clients. You are simply looking for as many potential customers as possible. The rest of the funnel will weed out people who are bad matches for your product, and leave you only with perfect fits. You need to cast the widest net possible at this stage, because the wider the top of the funnel becomes, the wider it will be at the bottom.

Let's assume you need to talk with one hundred people in order to find one client. If you only talk to twenty people a month, you will not find a new client for five months. In this case, by simply talking to five times more people, you can find a client every month. If you increase that to two or three hundred people a month, you can find two to three clients a month. This alone can exponentially increase your revenue.

The second stage of the funnel is **getting people to like you**. This is when we start narrowing the funnel down. We need to push out content that is attractive to our ideal client, whether that means sharing comic book pages, short stories, or articles about pandas.

Whatever you share, it should be hyper-targeted to your ideal client. If it is, then people who are interested in the things you are sharing will grow to like you. Meanwhile, people who aren't interested will drop out of your funnel before you invest too much energy in them.

This is the stage where people fall out of your funnel the most. You shouldn't be nervous when people unfollow you or unsubscribe from your mailing list at this point. My mailing list has a 31 percent unsubscribe rate in the first couple of weeks of somebody joining. I love that number because it means I'm weeding out the people who don't care about what I do.

This process of showing people what you do, building empathy with your ideal client, and weeding out ones who don't care about your message is one of the most powerful tools in business. Unfortunately, because of our natural need to be liked, we shy away from offending anybody. As a result, we try to please everybody and thus attract nobody.

Weeding out people who don't fit your product is a natural part of business. You shouldn't care about those people anyway, because they won't buy from you. Heck, they don't even like you. Your job isn't to please people who have no interest in what you are doing with your business. Your job is to connect with as many people as possible and let the right ones self-select to be part of your network over the long haul.

The third stage of the funnel is **making people trust you**. This is the trickiest part of the funnel. Everybody left at this stage of the funnel is in your ideal client pool. Now, you have to convince them to buy your product.

This is where your unique selling point and value proposition become essential. Even within your ideal client pool, there will be people looking for different features in their product.

Take a car for instance. Even among car buyers, some people want the most reliable vehicle for their family, others want a sports car with the fastest engine. Still others want the most luxurious ride on the road.

That's why car companies have multiple brands and models. There are many features people might want, and it's critical to target the right message to the right customer. If we didn't have different needs, then everybody would be driving around in the same beige Honda Accord, right?

But we aren't driving around in the same cars. There are more than a hundred different types of cars on the road, all with different features, sold by different companies, under different brands. They all capture a different part of the market. They all speak to a different type of person.

The same is true with your product. If you create high-end geek chic necklaces that cost $100 or more, then you are isolating yourself from people who are looking for cheap charms, and isolating yourself even more from people looking for an art print, or a comic book.

And that's natural. That's good. Heck, that's necessary to create a sustainable business. This is what finding the right client for your product is all about.

The final stage of the funnel is **people buying from you**. This is when the right customer is ready to make a buying decision and you have proven you are the right person to help them. Hooray! You've got a customer.

Notice there are three stages in this funnel before buying your product even comes into the equation. There will be people in your funnel who know you but won't like you, like you but won't trust you, and trust you but won't buy from you.

We can see this play out in our own lives. We all have a coworker we hate but can't get rid of, or a family member we love but wouldn't trust with a dollar of our money. We all have those people in our lives, but we also have a friend we would gladly give money to because we know they'll use our money to do something awesome.

The same is true with your business. Most people won't buy from you. When I go to a convention, I'm lucky if 1 percent of people sign up for my mailing list and 10 percent of those people ever buy from me. Even at a convention like San Diego Comic-Con, where I make thousands of dollars, I only sell a few hundred books and there are over 160,000 people in attendance.

But that's okay. In fact, that's how a funnel is supposed to work. This year we were set up in the small press area of San Diego Comic-Con, which meant people who came down our aisle self-identified as people who liked independent comic books. That already narrowed the field of potential customers down quite a bit.

From there, all I had to do was engage with as many people as possible so that some of them would like me, and some of *those* people would trust me, and then some of **those** people would buy from me.

In the end, by knowing how many people would attend the event, I could accurately predict how much I would make, and next year I can make an even more accurate prediction because I have even more data. This is the power of the funnel. If you understand how it works, you can predict the revenue for your entire business months into the future.

There is one more point I want to make before ending this section. When you start selling your work, a small number of people will buy from you immediately. This is because you have spent decades building up trust with certain people in your life. Those people have already worked their way to the bottom of your funnel and are ready to make a buying decision the moment you launch your storefront. Once those people work their way through the bottom of your funnel, though, there won't be anybody left to buy your product if you haven't built out the top of your funnel properly.

I've seen far too many creatives tell me that lots of people bought their book in the first month of release, but they haven't seen another a sale for over a year. This happens because they relied on their existing network to buy their product initially, and once those people flushed out of their funnel there was nobody to replace them. Remember, a funnel is only as good as the number of people you put into the top of it.

MODEL SUCCESS TO FEEL SUCCESSFUL

Most creative professionals don't like sales and marketing, because it feels too much like begging. People hate to beg. I hate to beg, too. I don't think anybody likes to beg; however, sales isn't about begging.

Do you ever think Starbucks begs for your money? Does it ever feel like begging when they post a billboard or run a TV spot?

Of course not. That would be crazy. Their marketing isn't begging, is it?

You bet it is. Every time they run an ad, they are saying, "Please come buy our coffee, because if you don't, we'll go bankrupt." Every time you see one of their billboards, they are pleading with you to spend just one dollar with them so they don't have to shut down their storefronts.

They aren't running those ads for the heck of it. They are running ads because they know begging for your money is essential to making their business successful. Starbucks spends millions of dollars a year begging for your money.

It never comes across as begging, though, does it? I've never once looked at a Starbucks ad and thought, "Wow. They must be desperate for my money."

And that's because Starbucks doesn't see it as begging. They see it as effective marketing. Effective marketing brings more money through the doors. They don't position their marketing as begging, so it doesn't come across as begging. They position their marketing as showing off their awesome stuff in the best light possible.

This is an important mindset shift you must employ to be successful as a creative professional. You must use marketing effectively, like Starbucks. But once we get over that mental block, how can we compete with a company like Starbucks whose marketing budget is astronomical?

That's the easy part. Starbucks is everywhere; their marketing is ubiquitous. While they won't ever tell you specific sales figures on a product, you can gauge effective marketing by how long a campaign runs and whether a product stays on their menu. Something like their pumpkin spice latte has very effective marketing.

The same is true in creative fields. Whether it's graphic design or publishing, there are billion-dollar players in your space spending millions of dollars on marketing every year. By studying them, you can model their success in your own business.

If you are a freelancer, there are individual creators who market themselves to acquire new business, as well. You can model their success just as easily as you can model the success of a company. All you have to do is follow their career and study their habits.

If you are trying to sell more prints at shows, look through the art books of successful show artists and mimic their price points. If you are a writer, study successful authors in your genre and find out what makes them special. If you want your work hung in a gallery, you can meet with fine artists to discover their process for getting a dealer.

All of this research is easily accomplished with a few days of studying. This isn't stealing, mind you. You aren't going to copy anything directly. You are simply getting a feel for how a successful person or company runs their business and then modeling their success in your own life.

This includes being on the same social media platforms, targeting the same users, and using similar color patterns in your logo to maximize your chances for success. Your goal is to take their successes (and their failures) and use them to quickly catapult your business beyond what you could do alone. If the average path to success takes ten years, you might be able to do it in eight, or even six, if you model success effectively.

If you aren't modeling success, then you are setting yourself up for failure. You will have to spend millions of dollars that you don't have on your own research. Then, you'll have to put brand new products on the market and play catch-up with those same companies that are already positioned better than you in the marketplace. It's a recipe for disaster.

By modeling successful players in your industry, you can move yourself ahead drastically with none of the upfront cost and very little time investment.

Additionally, if you model success, you will begin to feel successful. The more success builds in your own company, the more confident you will be in your own life…leading to more success.

EVERY SUCCESSFUL PERSON YOU KNOW IS A LOSER

We tend to look at somebody who is uber successful and only see the best days of their life. We see the time they won the Pulitzer Prize or an Oscar. We see the days they were booked on a television show or sold an important piece of art. We see the day they got a publishing deal or the day their book came out. We see every good moment in their lives, but those aren't the norm. The normal day of a successful person is filled with rejection and failure.

I'm here to tell you that every successful person you know is really a loser.

How is that possible? By definition they can't be a loser if they are successful, right? I mean, isn't the whole point of success that you are no longer a loser?

No.

If anything, the more successful you are, the bigger a loser you become.

Let's take Stephen King as an example. On average, Stephen King sells one to two million copies every time he releases a new book. He's arguably the most important and successful author of all time, with credits ranging from TV to novels to comic books, in multiple genres spanning multiple decades. By any measure, he's a massive success.

So, how can he be a loser? Let's look at those sales numbers in a different way for a moment, shall we? For the purpose of this discussion, let's assume he sells on the high side of his average and use the two million book number for his sales.

Now, let's talk about the world population. There are 7.4 billion people on this planet. Of those, 46.2 percent are at least fifteen years old. Even though I'm sure many younger people read his books, for the purpose of this discussion, I'm going to use fifteen as a barometer of his potential audience.

We also have to account for global illiteracy. Studies show 785 million people in the world suffer from illiteracy. If we take those people out of the potential audience pool, we are left with a possible 2.63 billion people in this world who could theoretically read Stephen King books, yet he only sells two million copies.

Therein lies the crux of why Stephen King is a loser. He sells a lot of books, but there are billions of people in his potential audience.

Think about those numbers for a moment.

Out of a possible 2,630,000,000 people, only 2,000,000 buy his books. While both of those numbers are huge, two million is only 10 percent of 1 percent of his potential readership.

If somebody told you that they had a 0.1 percent success rate selling their books, you wouldn't think them very successful, would you?

Of course not. A 0.1 percent success rate is terrible. Except that it's not for Stephen King. With the right scale, 0.1 percent could make you the most successful author on the planet.

Most creatives think successful people get every opportunity that comes their way, that everybody in the world loves their work, and that they can do no wrong. That's just not true. Most of a creative life, even at the highest levels, is abject failure and rejection.

As this example shows, only one in every thousand people read Stephen King books, and he's still massively successful. He has a global audience now, but he didn't always. When he began, he had an audience of one, and it grew from there.

That's where it starts, with just one person.

Every time you make a new work, you have the ability to grow that audience, and every time you meet somebody new, you have the chance to extend your audience a bit. Cherish those few people who love your work, because they don't come along often. Most people aren't going to be part of your audience.

You can't be discouraged by that. You can't be discouraged by rejection. You have to search for the one in a thousand people who will love your work and focus on them. Because in today's technological age, you can find those people easier than ever. It's not only possible, it's certain. If you give it enough time and energy, you will find your audience.

If you need to talk with a thousand people to find one potential customer for your work, then we should be able to agree that the quickest way to success is through scaling your message. You need to build a massive platform to be successful, because the larger your online and in-person presence, the more sales you will make, right?

It becomes a numbers game. How do you talk to a thousand people in the quickest way to build your audience the fastest? If that becomes your mentality, then the rejection falls away. All you then care about is finding your rabid fans, and every time somebody says "no," it just puts you closer to a "yes." It quickly becomes as important to put 999 people in the no pile as it is to find the one person to put in the yes pile.

If you can move your mentality toward this model, you will not be put off when you get a no, or even one hundred nos, because all you need is that one yes in a thousand to be successful. It's about ignoring those rejections and focusing on the yeses.

My golden rule of business is this: Anybody can find an audience. The only trick is whether you can find that audience before money runs out.

There is an audience for everything, but if you worry about the rejection, you'll never find yours. I very much doubt Stephen King cares about being a loser. He focuses on the wins, on the 0.1 percent of people who love his work, and he doesn't worry himself with the rest.

If you can do that, you might one day be as big a loser as Stephen King.

YOU CAN'T OUT-FAMOUS SOMEBODY, SO OUTWORK THEM

As a young creator, you will not have as many Instagram followers as Kim Kardashian; you can't expect to sell as many copies of a book as Neil Gaiman. You will not be able to sell a painting for as much as Banksy. There is no way you can expect to have as much success as they do with a single project. At least, not when you first start out.

Luckily, what you lack in audience you can make up for with tenacity. You can spend more of your day creating awesome stuff. What you lack in fame you can make up in sheer volume of output.

There are many Kindle authors who make a decent living because they release a new book every two months. There are artists on Etsy who are happy to sell a new product each day to make a living. These people are making a living by outworking Banksy. They put out so much content that the volume of it allows them to be successful.

My friend Rozine has almost 5,000 items in her Zazzle shop. That's a massive amount of inventory. It took an incredible amount of effort to build up that sort of catalog, but now it's done and she can sell them forever.

 What do you think the chances are that you could find something you wanted on her site? Pretty good, right? I would say it's almost impossible for somebody to leave her store without finding something they want to buy.

Let's put this into some cold, hard numbers for you.

If a successful year for you means that you've sold ten thousand books, there are many ways for you to hit that number. You could, of course, launch one book and sell ten thousand copies. That's the ideal because it means less work for you. It's probably not going to happen, though— at least not with your first book. Especially if it's self-published.

Luckily, that's not your only option for success. You could also sell one thousand copies of ten books, right?

It means you have to crank out one book almost every month, but you would hit the same sales numbers if you had ten times the product but sold one tenth the volume of each title. In the end, you are still making a living as a writer, you just have to massively increase your output.

My point is that the goal is not necessarily to sell ten thousand copies of one book. It's to sell ten thousand copies of your entire catalogue of books so you can live off your art and build a career.

That's at the core of what it means to outwork somebody to gain your own success. You might not be able to gain an audience as somebody who's already successful, but you can get more product in front of people. By sheer volume you can make a living.

THE VALUE OF SHOWING UP

Eighty percent of success is just showing up. I am the perfect depiction of this fact. When I lived in Washington, D.C., I stayed in my cocoon, convinced that the world would come to me if I just made something cool. After I moved to Los Angeles, I realized that I needed to meet people, mostly because nobody cared about what I was doing. So, I started going out to events and meeting new people.

At first, I knew nobody. I sat in a corner alone and had no friends. I didn't have anything but a few finished scripts, after all. Who would want to talk with me?

After a few events, I started meeting people who were further along on the path that I wanted to tread. I was nervous to talk with them, but after a couple of interactions I became more and more comfortable. I made a terrible first impression, but my third impressions were dynamite.

Because I kept showing up, I was able to make those third impressions on people who have since become great friends of mine. I learned so much during our interactions that it helped me decide to start making comics and writing books.

Once I made that decision, I went to conventions as an attendee and talked to people exhibiting behind the table. After all, they were exactly where I wanted to be. Meanwhile, I kept showing up at networking events and hanging out with creative people. I would show my new friends everything I was doing, get notes, and build goodwill with awesome people who were doing exactly what I wanted to do.

Over time, creators opened up to me just like you would with an old friend. By being nothing more than present and amiable, I moved past the acquaintance stage and formed real friendships with influential people who were only heroes and myths to me when we first met.

They started asking me questions instead of the other way around. Eventually, it became natural to know all the big players in comics and publishing; it became natural for me to talk about making stuff with these people because they were my friends. Not just acquaintances, but legitimate friends of mine.

When I finished project after project, it showed I was legit as a creator on top of being an awesome friend. The more projects I finished, the bigger my reputation grew within the creative community of people doing exactly what I wanted to do.

 Eventually, I started exhibiting my work at shows. Once I moved behind the table as an exhibitor, my career exploded. I already knew most of the players and now I was an authority. As I grew my company, people started pitching ideas to me instead of the other way around. I saw the wide eyes in their faces like mine had been so many years ago.

That all started, though, because I kept showing up to the right places until the right people accepted me as one of their own. It didn't happen overnight, but I kept showing up until it did.

Too many people don't show up, or stop showing up in a year because it's just too hard. There is a sort of extinction point for creatives. The extinction point is the moment when a creative vanishes off the face of the earth and you never see them again.

Not literally, of course. They're still alive, but they stop showing up to networking events, abandon online forums, and no longer attend conventions. They are out of the sight and mind out of the creative community, thus becoming all but extinct. If you can make it past the extinction point, you are suddenly taken much more seriously by the community as a whole.

I think it's because there are so many people who say they want to do a thing, like write a book or illustrate a comic…but then don't. If we took the time to invest in every one of these people, we'd be heartbroken all the time. The path to success is littered with people who wanted to do things and then stopped showing up. As you prove yourself by being around people and accomplishing cool things, people start to respect you and like you more, feeding your funnel more and more over time.

Think about your own life. Aren't there people who have become your friends simply because they kept coming around? I know it's happened to me. It's the same way in your creative life.

You don't have to do this in person either. You can show up in the right online forums and Facebook groups instead—some of my best creative friends live a world away.

Whether it's in person or in real life, the best thing you can do for your career is show up. That's essential. It takes no skill. It takes no talent. It just takes having the ability to be nice to people.

If you do nothing else but show up over a long enough time horizon with the right people, you can be successful. Of course, if you keep showing up and can make awesome stuff as well, then success is almost a guarantee.

ON PITCHING

If you want to get somebody interested in buying your product, whether it's a book, a print, or even your services, you need to start with a dynamite pitch.

In my experience, you don't have much time to catch somebody's interest. Luckily, I've perfected the steps to a good pitch so you can gain somebody's attention in a minimal amount of time. Once they're hooked, you can spend as much time as you want with them. The trick is getting them interested in the first place.

I've tailored this formula through dozens of shows, but it can be used on social media, in meetings, or basically anywhere you need to get somebody's attention.

A pitch needs to be simple and concise with specific appeals for your intended audience. There are tons of steps that go into a great pitch. Don't worry if you get frustrated with it. Pitching, like any art form, gets better with practice.

Step 1: The question

The first step in any good pitch is the question. This is where you get your potential customer to engage with you by answering a simple yes or no question.

My first question to passersby at a con is usually "Do you want to see a cool comic?" However, as the variety of titles at Wannabe Presses grows, my pitches vary depending on what I am trying to push on any given day. If I want to sell more of my murder mystery novel, the question is "Do you like murder?" If I am trying to sell kids' books, the question is "Wanna see something that will put your kid to sleep?"

The people who stopped and replied "yes" were immediately self-identifying that they were interested in what I was pitching. I knew they were in my target market because they said "yes."

One of the most important concept in sales is the idea that many small yeses lead to one big yes—the big yes being a sale. If you can get people to say "yes" over and over again, they are confirming their interest in your product, and you have positioned yourself well to win their business.

If you are selling yourself and not your product, your question might be, "Are you sick of freelancers that bail?" or "Are you having trouble making people notice your brand?" If you are selling prints, you might ask, "Are you looking for a new accent piece for your bedroom?" or "Are your walls annoyingly bare?"

You won't know exactly what works until you get out into the world and test several possibilities, but the idea is to get somebody to say "yes" to you right off the bat with a simple, innocuous question.

Step 2: The option

Once your potential customer is engaged with your pitch, you need to give them a simple two-choice option to move the conversation along to the next step. This option is another way to make your potential customer self-identify their preferences. When there are two comic books on my table, I ask "Do you like psychological mind screws or girls that kick butt?"

By giving them the choice, I've forced them to buy into their preference. Psychologically, this puts people in a more receptive mood to buy. By choosing their favorite, they agree they are interested in what I am selling. Now, all I have to do is make my case and hope they bite.

The beauty of this option is that I know every possible outcome and can plan my pitch accordingly. You know what your pitch will be if they say option one, and you know your pitch if they say option two. Even if they don't pick either option, you know your next step because you've limited their potential responses. For instance, if they say "both," or if they pause for more than a second, I always pitch my best seller.

Some people prefer to ask their customers open-ended questions, but that is a dangerous game. If you ask a question like "What are you shopping for today?" or "What do you like?" you are giving the power to the buyer. They could say anything. For all you know, they might say, "I'm here because goats are cool." By using the two-choice option, you get all the advantages of engagement with none of the risk posed by open-ended questions.

By narrowing down your potential customer's options, you can nail your pitch every time. With pitching, even a few seconds' delay can be the difference between a sale and the customer walking away in disgust.

Step 3: The pitch

Did you notice there are two steps before we even get to the pitch? This is called "priming the customer," and it allows for you to get a couple of yeses before you even pitch the product. It also forces the customer to self-identify as a member of your ideal audience—twice. This leads to a more engaged listener and higher overall sales.

Your pitch is a simple one-sentence summary of your project's biggest hook. This isn't a summary of what your product does, but an emotional appeal to your customer. People make purchases based on emotion, so you need to make an emotional connection to the buyer. The good news is they've already self-identified that they want to hear your pitch. Now, all you have to do is nail the emotional hook.

Emotional connection is a powerful thing, and it's the most powerful buying trigger you have to help boost your sales. When somebody doesn't know you, they must be able to connect with your product emotionally in order for you to make a sale.

Don't worry if you don't have this down perfectly at first. Discovering the emotional resonance of your product is difficult. You should write out ten to twenty potential pitches and then start delivering them to people to find the one with the best emotional connection. Most likely, you will need to combine the best parts of several pitches for the best effect.

Before a product ever even launches, I spend hundreds of hours developing the exact wording of its pitch. I show people our in-progress work, tell them as much as I can about it, and watch how they react, noting which parts of my description light them up. I mold that all into the perfect pitch. By the time the product launches, I know the exact emotional beats necessary to maximize sales.

Step 4: The flavor

Once you finish your pitch, let it settle in for a moment with your potential customer. Let them look at the product and turn it over a couple times. Once they've looked at it for a few seconds, you should start adding on some flavor elements to spice up your pitch. This is when you start peppering in some unique selling points and your value proposition for whatever you are selling.

These flavor elements are things they can't find easily by looking at your product, like where it was made, why you made it, or who worked on it with you. Every product is different, and you need to find the right "spice" to resonate with a product's ideal audience.

For my graphic novel, *Ichabod Jones: Monster Hunter*, people respond when I tell them about our influences for making the book, that we used a single artist for everything, and that it's a complete story. With *Katrina Hates the Dead*, I know they respond when I talk about the artist going on to work on a *Star Wars* story and that we have additional process images in the back showing how we made the book. Each of these bits of flavor perk up the reader and strengthen their desire to buy the product.

Step 5: The acceptance

Before you ask for the sale, you want to get them to agree once again that the product is cool. This can be as simple as "Pretty cool, right?" You are priming them one more time before asking them to buy. They've agreed this is a product they want—three times—and now it's time to ask for the sale.

Step 6: The ask

Ask for the business by stating the price of your services and giving them another optional close. For instance, you could say, "This book is twenty dollars or two for thirty," or "Will that be cash or charge?" This final optional close once again primes the customer that they are going to buy. Instead of the option being yes or no, it's, "How do I want to pay?"

Don't be too pushy here. You'll see their reaction when you state the price. Most people will back off, some will buy, and some will be on the fence. For the people who back off, exchange cards and add them to your mailing list. For the people who buy, have them pay and add them to your mailing list. For the people on the fence, move on to step seven.

Step 7: Objection handling

Most people aren't going to buy your project. Some will flat out say no, but others will sit on the fence waiting for you to convince them to buy. They want your product but you haven't given them a strong enough reason to give you their hard-earned money. So, you have to give them a good reason to buy.

With these people, you want to give them another question, like "What's stopping you from buying this right now?" However, a better question would be, "I know you want this, but you're trying to save your money to see if there is something better, right?"

They will almost always agree with this, and then you can make them a special offer, something like, "What if I gave you a money-back guarantee? If you find something better at this con, come back and I will give you your money back." I've been making this offer for years, and nobody has ever come back to get their money back.

Maybe they will have a great reason, like "I'm not getting paid for two weeks." Maybe they have a crappy reason you can easily overcome and make them a customer. Perhaps the pricing is too high, and in that case you can lower the price slightly, or maybe they really want multiple pieces, in which case you can offer them bundle pricing.

If you can overcome these objections in one round of objection handling, then you should have a customer on your hand. If they still have objections, try to flush them out with one more round before giving up.

You want to do at most two rounds of this objection handling. If you can't make a sale by then, exchange cards, add them to your mailing list, and make them a future prospect. You can keep going for as long as you want with objections, but I've found if you can't convince them with two chances, then they most likely won't buy, at least not until later.

In practice, this entire pitch, from meeting a customer through objection handling, takes no more than a couple of minutes, max. It's the whittling down everything you want to say into a couple sentences that takes forever. The actual pitch should be no more than two minutes.

The first time you do it, it won't take two minutes. It will take forever, and you'll get everything wrong. You'll sound terrible. You'll say things in the wrong order. You'll say things you didn't mean to say. You'll ramble on forever. You'll be...just awful.

That's okay.

It's unnatural to talk about your project. Nobody likes to do it. Since you don't want to do it, either, you'll stop after two or three attempts. Then, you'll hang your head in shame and never want to do it again.

Don't give up.

That's the key to this. You can't stop. You have to keep going. Over time you will get better. The more you practice your "pitching muscle," the better you'll get and the more natural you will become. The key to a pitch is that it can't sound like a pitch. It has to sound natural, and it can't sound natural until you've done it a thousand times. You can't do it a thousand times if you stop after the first attempt.

You're supposed to suck at this at first. Sucking at something, as Jake the Dog from *Adventure Time* says, is the first step to being kind of good at something. If you want to be kind of good at pitching, you have to do the work. There are no shortcuts in coming up with and practicing a compelling pitch. The only secret is to do it a whole bunch of times.

IDEAL CLIENT AVATARS

We've touched on the concept of ideal client avatars throughout this book, but now it's time we officially defined the term and discussed it at length. While "ideal client avatar" sounds like marketing gibberish, it's one of the most important principles to understand if you want to build a career in the arts—or any career, frankly.

An ideal client avatar represents the person who most resonates with your message and is thus incredibly likely to buy your product. It is the virtual representation of your perfect customer.

There are two factors that come into play which help determine your ideal client avatar. The first factor is somebody who has a very high **customer lifetime value**. The second factor is a person with a very low **customer acquisition cost**.

Customer lifetime value is the amount somebody will buy from you over the course of their life. Your ideal customer will be the type of person who spends at least a hundred dollars on your products every year. This is a concept made famous by Kevin Kelly, the founding executive editor of *Wired*. Kelly wrote a piece on his blog in 2008 called "1,000 True Fans," which became one of the definitive pieces on building an audience with its claim that if an artist can find one thousand people willing to spend one hundred dollars a year on their work, then they can successfully make a living on their art. I hope we can all agree that generating $100,000 of income would make a very successful year.

Conversely, **customer acquisition cost** is the amount of money it costs to find a new customer and make a sale. Between tabling at conventions, sending mailing list updates, advertising, and all of the other monetary outlays that come part and parcel with finding a client, the less we spend acquiring a client means we make more money at the end of the day.

Simply put, your ideal client avatar is the person most receptive to your message and the person with whom you most want to speak.

It has to be both.

There will be people you want to speak with who have no interest in your message, and people who want to hear your message that you don't care about at all. The ideal client avatar is the beautiful merging of these two points.

So…how do we find our ideal client avatar?

First, we must find the type of people who inspire us to create. This will take some deep reflection, but you know there is a person in your life who will love your product more than anybody else. This doesn't have to be your family. It can be a friend or even somebody you aren't that close with, though I highly recommend staying inside your close friend circle at first.

Have you thought of somebody? Good. Then, let's build an avatar.

To start forming our ideal client, we need to test whether that person will be the right fit to buy what you are trying to sell. Remember, just because you want to make products for somebody doesn't mean your products will resonate with them.

To find out if somebody is a good fit, we have to stalk their Facebook feeds for a while to see what kinds of stuff they like. We need to make sure they are buying what you are selling. If you want to make death metal pins and they are buying fluffy bunny plushes, you are barking up the wrong tree and need to start over.

Once you are relatively confident that they buy the same type of stuff that you want to make, it's time to interview them. It doesn't have to be anything formal, but you want feedback about why they buy what they buy. Do they like bright colors or are they more into texture? Does size matter? What is it that resonates with them when they buy something?

After you have that interview, it's time to make some different products and show them to your ideal client. This is why using an immediate friend or family member is easiest, because they will be open and receptive to looking at your product. This is also why it's best not to pick your mother or anybody who will automatically love anything that you do. You want real and honest feedback about whether you are doing something that resonates with your ideal client.

This interview isn't about selling your product, but you need to know if they would buy what you are trying to sell. If you can't tell whether or not they would buy your product, push harder. This is critical research and if you get it wrong then your business will suffer and you will have to start again. You don't want to build the wrong customer avatar.

Once you've done your research, it's time to rock and roll into mass production, right? Absolutely and unequivocally not.

You don't want to go into mass production just yet. After you have a good idea that your work will resonate with the right person, you need to find other people who will also be perfect fits for your product. This is the beginning of the ideal client avatar.

Create a profile of your ideal client based on your initial research. This profile needs to be as complete as you can make it. Your ideal client avatar should feel like a real person who lives and breathes. Your profile of them should include name, age, ethnicity, interests, personality traits, favorite foods, favorite TV shows, favorite movies, favorite bands, favorite websites, and anything else you can think of to make your avatar feel like a real person.

Once you have the profile created, use it to find five to ten other people who fit your ideal client avatar. Replicate the same process you used before. Interview your potential customers and show them your product just you like did with the original person.

Some of the assumptions you made about your ideal client will be correct and some will be wildly misinformed. That's okay. That's how it should be. Use the new data you collected from these interviews to recreate your ideal client avatar and focus it more clearly. Your avatar will now become more complete and fleshed out, because you have five to ten times the research data.

After finding five to ten people who love your product, it's time to test your ideal client avatar on people you don't know.

To do this, you need to create a small batch of products. Then, find a craft fair, comic convention, or job fair where your ideal client avatar exists in the real world. Bring your products to this event. Find people who resemble your ideal client and see if they rabidly buy what you are selling.

If they do, use your new data to compile a more complete customer avatar. If they do not, analyze why they are not buying your product, make corrections to your avatar, and try again. The more people you speak with, the more complete and real your customer avatar will become.

The stronger your ideal client avatar, the more you will be able to focus on creating a product for the right kind of person, lowering your customer acquisition cost, and increasing your lifetime customer value. Then, you can use all that data to find more people who fit that profile, which is the key to scaling your creative business.

BRING THE PASSION

The single best way to convince somebody to buy your work is through passion. I often joke that 10 percent of my sales come from passion alone.

As I've stated before, we are emotional creatures and we make purchases based on emotion. An artist who is able to convey passion for their work through their actions, their voice, and their words, will have a much easier time getting sales because they can hit an emotional chord with their audience.

When I first started selling products I talked in a very low voice. I didn't have any emotion behind my words. I gave the facts about what the product I was selling did, but never conveyed why customers should buy it. I had absolutely no passion and it showed.

Consequently, my sales numbers sucked, and yours will too if you can't bring your passion to the forefront. If you can't get excited and passionate about your product, how can anybody else get passionate about it enough to buy it?

You are your best advocate. You need to love your project 110 percent to succeed. But more than love it, you need to convey to other people why you love it. After I learned that, I went from a below average salesperson to a superstar.

I know you have passion for what you do. If you didn't, then you would be doing something else, something easier. Nobody creates things because of the money. It's passion that drives artists. Passion is often buried deep down in the recesses of our soul. It's our job to pull it out and convey it to the world.

So, how do we seize our passion? Here are a couple of strategies that work. Don't feel the need to try all of them at once. This is a slow, gradual process that takes months or years to work through.

Write about why you want to create. The most important part of bringing your passion to the forefront is figuring out the real reasons you create. These are the internal motivations that make you passionate for what you do. Why do you sit up at night or early in the morning making your projects? Why do you forego time with loved ones—and sleep—to sit in solitude in front of a computer? What makes you want to create art instead of working on something with more stability?

Focus your general passion onto specific projects. Once you have the overall reasons behind your creative drive, look through your projects and determine why you were passionate to make each specific piece. You can't say, "I don't know. I just did." That's not a good enough reason to spend sixteen hours on a print. Or if that is the reason, you shouldn't be focusing your sales on that piece. People buy based on the passion displayed on the page as much as the passion you convey through your sales actions. There has to be a driving force behind why a piece needed to get out into the world in order to make it a success.

Practice talking about the passion behind your projects. After discovering why you are passionate about a project, it's time to practice on real people. Assemble a group of creators and take turns talking through why each of you are passionate about specific projects. Hearing their passions will help you better define yours. This can't be a one-time thing. You need a standing date to talk about your projects to make your deep-seated passion bubble to the surface. The more you talk about your project, the more your passion will intensify and focus until it's honed into a finely tuned laser that can cut through the noise of life and connect powerfully with your ideal customers.

Study professional salespeople. Go to YouTube and find popular presentations salespeople have made to audiences through the years. I'm not just talking about product launches, either. Even TED and XOXO are basically sales presentations, although their purpose is to sell an idea instead of a product. There are multiple sales styles, as varied as the sales people themselves, but any effective salesperson can truly convey the passion behind their work. You don't have to be the Sham-Wow guy. Steve Jobs was equally effective in communicating his passion to an audience. Your job is to find the sales style you admire and then model everything that makes that style successful.

Work on your body language. Body language says everything without saying anything. If your head is down, your voice is low, and your body is drooped into itself, you will come across as sad and dispassionate to your intended audience. If you can look up, smile, and push your shoulders back, you will come across confident and passionate to everybody, including yourself. Model the sales style you found in step four. Notice the body language of the people who use it and how it works to convey their message.

Create a persona. In real life, I'm a miserable curmudgeon with a low, monotonous voice and I hate to smile. But when I go to a con I'm a bubbly, smiling fool with a higher octave, engaging voice. What people see in public is not who I really am at home. They see the persona I've created to make the public like me and want to buy my products. I force my voice half an octave higher, because people find higher voices more pleasant to the ears and less intimidating. I smile because people prefer buying from people in a good mood. I make sure to vary my pitch and tone, because people are turned off by monotony. I worked hard on the worst parts of my personality, the parts people didn't like, until they turned into strengths. Then, I turned those strengths into a persona I use to engage with the public. This isn't lying. It's molding your personality so it's the best reflection of yourself.

Try it out. Once you have a fully realized persona and know the "why" behind your passion, it's time to try it out on the world. Don't worry if it doesn't feel natural at first. Conveying your passion naturally takes time. The most important part is not to give up. People can forgive a lot of flaws if you just show a massive amount of passion for what you do.

Passion is one of the most important tools in any salesperson's toolkit. Making great content is essential, but showing enthusiasm for your project is what sets you apart. Anybody can talk about the whats and the hows of their work, but what really matters to customers is *why* you do what you do.

If you can make an emotionally impassioned plea for why you love your work, you'll be able to make your potential customers love it too—and if they love it, they'll be more likely to buy it.

STANDING OUT FROM THE CROWD

Do you know why there are so many sequels and remakes on the market today? Yes, they are safe bets, but do you know why they are safe bets? It's because things that were made decades ago stand out more in the public's mind. Why is that? Because they had less competition vying for our attention.

A million books will hit the market this year. A million. Two hundred years ago, there wasn't a fraction of a fraction of a fraction of that number. Therefore, *Alice in Wonderland* had a much better chance of being remembered for generations to come—people had fewer choices back then.

When television first exploded onto the market in America there were only three channels. Because of that lack of choice, everybody watched one of those channels, even if they didn't like any of the programming. Therefore, more people remember content from previous generations, even if it's not as good as what's available now.

Today, content is plentiful. There is more information created in one month than was available in the entirety of pre-internet history combined. That means the ability to stand out amongst a sea of content is harder today than it ever was before. Yet it is no less imperative.

The secret to standing out is doing what the next person won't. Let me give you an example. There are roughly 242 million adults living in America today. Studies show about 50 percent of those adults want to write a book. That means at any given time there are 121 million people in America who want to write a book.

Out of that 121 million people, there are roughly one million books published every year. Just by actually writing a book and publishing it, you have stood out above 120 million adults living in America who will never finish their manuscript.

One million is still a huge number, though. Nobody wants to compete with a million people. How about we narrow that down further with an example? These aren't the exact numbers or percentages you can expect to find in the field. I'm only using them to prove my point.

Let's say that out of the one million books published every year, only half of the authors have published more than one project. Well, if you published multiple books you would stand out from the people that just have one, right? Of course you would. You would have distinguished yourself above half of the books on the market and narrowed your competition from a million to a pool of just 500,000.

If only half of those people have copies available in paperback form, you can narrow your competition pool to only 250,000 people simply by offering a paperback version of your book.

That's still a ton of people, but 250,000 is way less than 121 million, right? Of course it is. They're much better odds, but it's still too many people for my taste.

Luckily, we can cut our competition much further than that. Out of the 250,000 who have paperback version of their books, no more than 10 percent of them will have more than ten thousand social media followers. Therefore, if you can build a large internet presence, you are now only competing with just 25,000 people.

Out of that 25,000 people, only 50 percent will construct a high-quality website. If you create a quality website, you are competing with just 12,500 people. Only half of them will build a mailing list with more than a thousand people on it. If you can build a mailing list that size, you are competing with just 6,750 people.

Finally, out of those 6,750 people, only 10 percent of those people will shell out the money to exhibit at conventions. If you are willing to spend the money to exhibit at shows, you have cut your competition from 121 million down to just 675 people. Those are way better odds! And you can keep narrowing your competition over and over again until you are in competition with absolutely nobody but yourself.

This doesn't just apply to books, either. You can set yourself apart like this in any creative pursuit in any field. The key is researching your market and finding what sets the best performers apart from the competition.

Standing out is about doing what the next person will not do in order to rise above the clutter. The more things you can do to stand out above the crowd, the more resonance your message will have and the more opportunities you have to make sales because you are in competition with fewer people.

THE FOUR TYPES OF OFFERS YOU NEED

Every product is priced differently. I can't tell you exactly how to price yours. Pricing depends on whether your work is a print or an original, how long it takes to create, and the mass market viability of what you are trying to sell. You need research data on comparable products to find out what the market will bear. Luckily, there are places like Etsy, Amazon, and Kickstarter, which are great research tools to find comparable products in your market space.

That being said, I can tell you that there are four types of offers you need before you can enter the marketplace effectively. These four types of offers have been tested rigorously in all sorts of market conditions and always bear out successfully. I have found them incredibly effective in all types of creative fields, from book sales to prints and even informational products.

Offer #1: Freebies – Freebies are critically important to getting noticed in the market. Most people think of freebies as business cards and fliers. While those are important, they're not the freebies I'm talking about. In this scenario, what you want are nicely created, yet simple to make, pieces that can be given away for free in exchange for an email address.

Your most effective marketing is still an email newsletter. People guard their email addresses with their lives. If you want them to part with their email and join your community, you need to offer them something nice, which makes you synonymous with quality.

These freebies don't have to be expensive or labor intensive to make. You can offer a branded button, sticker, or print in exchange for an email address. It can even be something you usually offer for under five dollars, but are willing give it away for free if somebody signs up for your mailing list.

The key to this is the exchange of free merchandise for an email address. An email address is incredibly valuable, as is your freebie. When people give away their email address, they are giving away something of value to them, and you should make sure you respect that value by giving them something well crafted.

I have successfully offered prints, buttons, and free digital comics in exchange for an email address. Alterna Comics has an amazing freebie offer of thirty free digital comics for joining their mailing list. Your goal is to provide incredible value for freebies so that signing up is a no brainer. Then, when you deliver incredible quality people will think, "Wow. This is what they offer for free? Their paid content must be incredible!"

Whatever you do, do not give these freebies away without getting that email address. If you give your work away for free, then you are unnecessarily devaluing it. Exchanging your work for an email address, however, psychologically forces the customer to place a value to your work as well, even if that value is only their email.

Offer #2: The Tripwire offer – The tripwire offer is intended to turn somebody who has been lurking around your store gathering freebies into a paying client. These are low-priced items (under ten dollars) which act as the gateway drug into spending loads more with you in the future.

If your core business is twenty-dollar art prints, then a five-dollar print would be a good tripwire offer. Similarly, if you are selling books, a digital version for five bucks would be a good tripwire offer. If you are selling your services as a sculptor, a quick one-inch statue for ten bucks would be a good tripwire offer.

We've all had the experience of joining a mailing list. We keep getting emails for a long time without paying a dime. We think about unsubscribing, but the content is just valuable enough that we don't. Then, one day the mailing list offers a product that has such an incredible value we have to try it. After that, we are hooked into spending tons of money, because we finally recognize the value of their product and we'll shill out money for it.

This is my wife's experience with BetaBrand. She lurked around their mailing list for ages until she finally bought something for cheap. The product ended up being incredible. Now, she spends hundreds of dollars a year on their products. This would not have happened if she wasn't offered a cheap offer to test their incredible products first.

The point of a tripwire offer is to provide something beautifully made at an incredible value, so that people find it a no brainer to buy your higher-priced items in the future.

The biggest customer transition in your business is convincing somebody to move from a "lurker" to spending even one dollar on your brand. Once they spend that dollar, they are likely to spend much more if you can prove the value of your product.

Offer #3: Your Core Product – Your core product is the centerpiece of your business. Most creative businesses price their core product in the twenty to fifty-dollar range, but these core products can be incredibly expensive as well.

The core offer for a car dealership will be several thousands to even millions of dollars.

The core offer is what keeps the lights on in your business, and it is what you are pushing on your website and through the rest of your sales strategy.

Offer #4: Profit maximizer – If core products are the base of your sales, then a profit maximizer is the cherry on top. This offer has a slightly misleading name, as it deals more with increasing overall revenue than strictly targeting profits, but every additional dollar spent on your business should increase both revenue and profit margin simultaneously.

The idea of this offer is to increase the total amount customers spend on your products by adding additional products and services to your client's purchase during the checkout process. While adding potential clients to your sales funnel is crucial to the success or your business, encouraging your existing customers to spend more with each transaction is a fantastic way to immediately improve your bottom line.

This offer comes in all shapes and sizes. It might be asking your client to add an additional print to their order, or it could be adding additional services like website hosting to your current website design packages, or it could be asking customers to add the digital version of your book to their cart for a nominal fee. All of these offers increase the amount spent by your customers during each transaction, thus increasing your overall revenue.

Of course, the best profit maximizers are pure profit. My favorite profit maximizer during a Kickstarter campaign is offering a special thanks in the back of a book. This reward costs fifty dollars instead of twenty for just the book, and it takes almost no additional time, energy, or cost to implement. This additional reward is almost 100 percent profit. Meanwhile, it builds engagement with my audience, because they have become part of the book forever.

These four offers form the basis of any good sales strategy, whether it is in person or online. If you can nail these offers, you'll bring the most people to the top of your funnel while maximizing your sales when they reach the bottom and become clients.

MULTIPLE STREAMS OF REVENUE

Developing multiple streams of income is a critical factor to succeeding as an artist. Every product you release will be a new stream of income for you; every new stream of income will increase your potential revenue.

Your creative career is filled with potential income streams, from offering commissions, to creating charms, to licensing characters, to creating books, to freelancing for companies, and many others. The more potential streams of income you develop, the more stable your career will become.

While creating new products can generate additional income streams, so can creating brand new companies that don't have anything to do with your art. I've owned a Verizon dealership since I began Wannabe Press. It has nothing to do with creativity, but it still accounts for a substantial part of my monthly income while allowing me the freedom and flexibility to follow my passions.

The dealership took a lot of time to set up, but eventually I transitioned my business so it's run exclusively by freelance reps. In short order, that business has gone from requiring twenty to thirty hours of my time each week into a passive income stream I deal with for under four hours every month.

If you are thinking about leaving your job to pursue your art full time, you should start looking for ways to immediately generate additional income streams that can act as replacement income for your current job. A good replacement income should make you at least a thousand dollars per month profit while requiring less effort than your current job.

Here's a real-world scenario of how this works:

Let's say you make $52,000 a year for working a standard forty-hour work week. That means you make a thousand a week, or a thousand for every forty hours worked.

If you can create a company that generates a thousand dollars in profit per month while only needing ten hours of time commitment, then you've gained back thirty hours to work on your creative pursuits.

If you could find three additional income streams that account for a total of four thousand dollars in profit, but only take forty hours total to manage, then you've decreased your time commitment by 75 percent and are still making the same amount of money.

Does that make sense? In your current job, it would take you one hundred and sixty hours of time to accumulate four thousand dollars. In this scenario, you would make the same four thousand in just forty hours, giving you one hundred and twenty additional hours of time to pursue your art.

What would one hundred and twenty more hours do for your artistic life? What would you do with that much freedom? How much further could your business go with that many additional hours to funnel into it?

In the end, your goal should be to find ten stable streams of income that each account for 10 percent of your overall monthly income. Then, you are only ever at risk of losing one tenth of your income at any one time if something goes wrong.

These streams can be additional businesses, new products, or offering additional services. The more the merrier when it comes to income streams. It's even better to have one hundred streams of income that each account for one hundredth of your income, and having a thousand streams is better still.

The fewer income streams you have, the less stable your overall revenue. If you only have three streams, and each one accounts for 33 percent of your income, you risk of a third of your income drying up at any one time. Losing 10 percent of your income sucks, but losing a third of your income is devastating.

These income streams don't evolve overnight. If you work them right, though, they can be the difference between struggling in a job that saps your energy, stressing because you only have one income stream, and transitioning into a full-time creative career.

THE TWO LEVERS THAT CONTROL YOUR CASH FLOW

There are two levers which control every business. They are the only two levers that matter when it comes to creating positive cash flow, which is something we all want. Before we get into the levers, let's talk about cash flow for a moment. So, what is cash flow?

Cash flow is the amount of cash moving into, out of, and through your business. Positive cash flow means that you have more money coming into your business than going out of it, leading to profit.

The opposite is true of negative cash flow. Negative cash flow means more money is going out of your business than coming into it. Most companies face negative cash flow for the first two or three years of their life cycle, if not more.

Negative cash flow does not necessarily mean your business is failing. It might mean you are rapidly trying to grow your business through advertising, marketing, more expensive con tables, inventory printing, or any other expenses that are part of your long-term plan.

Wannabe Press was in negative cash flow for all of 2015 and most of 2016, because we kept having to buy books in bulk, pay for increasingly expensive con tables, and extend ourselves with marketing efforts to improve our brand recognition. That negative cash flow wasn't fun, but it helped cement our inventory reserves and brand recognition for the future. Negative cash flow isn't horrible as long as you have the cash to burn and it's not a permanent situation.

Most people don't think of creating positive cash flow when it comes to their business. They believe that all cash flow leads to more money in the bank. Unfortunately, making more money usually comes with extra expenses. People tend to raise their expenses to their income level.

There are always nice things to have for your business that you can't afford at the moment, which having more money can allow you to buy. These could be things like producing more content, hiring staff, or putting a freelancer on retainer. These additional expenses don't enter into your mind until you have the revenue to pay for them. Once you do, though, that extra revenue flies out the door and leaves you no better than you were before.

At Wannabe Press, we kept increasing our revenue exponentially, yet we engaged with new vendors, bought bigger tables, started making new content, and hired more freelancers. All of these things ended up being extremely expensive and at the end of the day—even though we had more revenue—we actually ended up with far less money in the bank.

This is where the two levers come into your business. If you can understand these two levers, you'll always be able to improve your financial situation. The goal of these levers is to utilize them and make money appear whenever you need it. These two levers are the **pull lever** and a **push lever.**

Imagine the **pull lever** like a slot machine that is always ready to dispense money for you. If you can understand this lever, you'll be able to pull it and money will magically flow out. Every business makes money differently and until you understand exactly how your business rakes in the dollars, you'll be throwing haymakers trying to make more money.

This is what happened to me in 2015. I was trying everything from Amazon to Facebook ads and nothing worked. I was flailing and failing to make money in my business. It wasn't until I sat down at the end of 2015 and figured out exactly how we made money that I could pull the first lever at will and make money magically come out the other end. This lever needs to be so focused that it becomes your own personal piggy bank.

When I need to make money quickly now, I know I need to release a new product or go to a convention. In either case, I pull the first lever and money streams into my bank account. It's a fantastic relief to know exactly how I can make money whenever I need it.

The pull lever is what most people think about when it comes to having more money inside their business; however, the **push lever** is even more important in many respects. Think of a push lever like the wall of a dam. When you are spending too much money, you can push that lever and the dam shuts, leaving more money inside your business.

While the pull lever is essential for a successful business's growth, the push lever is essential to sustain your business. Once you start making revenue, your natural instinct is to spend every dollar that comes into your business. The push lever allows you to take a step back, analyze what you really need, and slow down expenses so you have money at the end of the month.

Let's take a real-world scenario.

You need to buy a new printer that costs a thousand dollars. Most people immediately place their hand on the pull lever, but if you only make one hundred dollars every time you pull that lever, you'll have to pull it ten times if you want to buy that printer. That's a lot of work.

Meanwhile, you might be buying coffee every day from Starbucks and going out to the bar every night with friends. Combined, this costs you five hundred dollars a month. By utilizing the push lever to halt those expenses, you can shut those flood gates and save five hundred bucks a month almost immediately. Then, you only have to utilize your pull lever five times, cutting your work in half. Or you can never pull that lever and make an extra thousand in two months.

Whether you utilize the pull lever, the push lever, or a combination of both, you know exactly how you will come up with the money without panicking. When you understand these two levers, the panic that exists inside most businesses fades away, because you always know how to make money when you need it.

BUYING TRIGGERS

The good news with sales is that people want to buy things. They actually want to help businesses succeed and find cool stuff in the process. The problem is that people are also inherently lazy and skeptical of the unknown. The key to sales is making sure a customer's desire to help out and to find cool products outweighs their laziness and skepticism.

One way to effectively overcome laziness is through the use of buying triggers. Buying triggers have been used by every company that has ever existed to build their brand. Once you learn about buying triggers, you will see them everywhere. (This is a bit like seeing the code underneath the Matrix.)

There are six essential buying triggers which have stood the test of time. They work in any creative field with any set of potential customers.

Commitment – When somebody willingly commits to joining your community, they are more likely to buy your product. This is the main value to people joining your mailing list, or wearing a button, or even taking a flier. They make a commitment when performing that action. It signifies they are part of your community. The more actions they take, the more commitment they build.

Every time they open a newsletter from you and don't unsubscribe, they are affirming that commitment. Every time they like one of your tweets or share a Facebook post, they are affirming their commitment to your brand again and again. The more you can enforce that commitment through words and actions, the more likely you are to have an enthusiastic ambassador for your brand—one who buys all your stuff.

Reciprocity – When you do something nice for somebody, they want to help you. That's just human nature. Knowing this, you need to provide value for your potential customer before you ever ask for a sale. Once you have provided incredible value through advice or some sort of free content, then people will gladly give you money, because you have helped them and treated them like a human being.

Social Proof – Human beings want to be part of the "in" crowd. If you can prove that other people are using your product, everybody else will want to use it, too. The hardest sales to make at conventions are the first ones. Once there are people running around the show floor with your product, other people are more likely to want it, as well.

Your work becomes valuable to a customer because other people saw the value in it already. People want to buy what their peers bought. They don't want to be left out in the cold. If you can show your customer that people they like and respect use your product, then you are more likely to convince them to buy it, too.

Scarcity – When you limit the available quantity of a product, customers become increasingly likely to make a buying decision in the moment. People believe products will be around forever and that they can always buy it later. When they realize a product is in limited supply, they are forced to make an immediate decision. This works wonders for people sitting on the fence about buying your product and also for people who desperately want your product but need a little push to finally take action.

Authority – If you can demonstrate that you are an expert in your field, people are more likely to buy your product over somebody else's. This is how you stand out above every other creative doing exactly what you do. They choose you because you are an expert in your field.

To prove your expertise, it's important to have consistently high-selling products for a long time, and it helps if you're able to teach other people how to do what you do. Another way is to write guest posts on other blogs, share your work on podcasts, or speak on panels. You can also use platforms like Medium and Kickstarter to build expertise, as the platform's authority can be transferred to you.

Liking – If somebody has a positive connection to you, they are more likely to buy from you. Think about it: You are more inclined to buy from somebody you like than somebody you don't care about, right? Of course you are.

The truth is that 10 percent of people will like you, 10 percent of people will hate you, and 80 percent will feel nothing for you. Your job is to focus on selling to the 10 percent who like you, while nudging some of that 80 percent from indifference toward liking you.

All of these buying triggers are essential for the long-term growth of your business. They are powerful on their own, but if you can mix them together, you will increase your sales exponentially.

Some of these triggers take time to build into your business—authority and social proof won't happen overnight. Others, like scarcity and commitment, you can build into your sales funnel today. Even if it takes time to seed some of these triggers into your business, it's important to have a plan to incorporate every one of them eventually.

PART 3

BUILDING AN AUDIENCE FROM SCRATCH

Now that we've covered the basics of sales, it's time to dig deep into building your audience from scratch. You'll learn the fundamentals about why people would want to join your audience and all of the elements necessary to supercharge your audience growth.

I'm going to assume for the purposes of this section that you have an audience of zero right now. Well, maybe you have some friends and family, but nobody else knows who you are…yet.

Most people who have explosive growth start with some sort of unfair advantage: maybe they worked as an executive for Merrill Lynch so they can build on that ingrained authority; they have a rich uncle who can feed them money to place Facebook ads until they succeed; maybe they wrote assignments from Marvel or Random House and can leverage that brand to build their own.

I assume none of that is true about you.

Before I launched Wannabe Press, I couldn't pay people to publish my work. It wasn't until I bypassed the naysaying companies and spoke directly to my audience that things started happening for me. It's the tips, tricks, and strategies I share in this section that grew my brand from nothing into a little army of Wannabes.

If there's one thing I'm proud of in my career, it's that I built a name for myself one person at a time. I did it without working for a big company. I didn't have a trust fund or a famous father. I didn't have any connections. Trust me, it can be done. With grit and determination, you can build an audience from the ground up, too.

This section is about how you—with no money, no audience, and no clients—can build a cohesive brand, make connections, and get people to buy into your company. If there's one thing I know about audience building, it's that anybody can build an audience for just about anything in this crazy, interconnected world…and you can, too.

VALUE FIRST

When it comes to building an audience, the first thing we must do is develop the right perspective on how successful businesses operate. Most people run their business with a "buy first" mentality. Their concern begins and ends with a customer buying their product and finding the value after they have it in their hands.

Unfortunately, that perspective is antithetical to building a large audience. If people just wanted to buy a product and jet, they would head to Amazon and find the cheapest option. Honestly, that's what most people will do anyway.

If there's any hope of competing against behemoths like Amazon, we must think of building an audience in a new way. We must think of our customers as human beings with wants and needs and start providing value to their lives before we ever ask for a sale. We need to ask ourselves, "What would my ideal audience like to know about?" and then deliver that value to them in spades.

The best example I can think of in the creative space is Jim Zub. Jim is a writer who broke through with the creator-owned book, *Skullkickers,* from Image Comics. He's since gone on to write for Marvel and Dynamite, among others. He produces some of the best books on the market today, but without his "value first" mentality, I never would have picked up a single one of Jim's books.

I remember the first time I started having a connection to Jim's work. I knew about *Skullkickers* in theory, but had never read a single issue. My connection didn't come from reading one of his books either. It came from a blog post.

A friend of mine posted a blog Jim wrote which detailed exactly how much money he made from *Skullkickers*. It had graphs, charts, and was packed with insights borne from working in the trenches of comics.

He detailed the painstaking losses and the gains he made to break even. It was an incredible and insightful look at the economics of independent comic books. I was immediately hooked on his work, and I had never even read a page of his comics. I trusted him because he served my needs and never asked for anything in return.

He didn't have to do that.

He could have just gone on like most other creatives and hoarded his secrets. Yet he didn't. He gave away his best information, because he wanted to provide value to the audience he was trying to serve. By posting that blog and others like it, he gained immense goodwill with his audience and stood out in an overcrowded marketplace.

Over time, people started finding him at shows and bought his book because he helped them so much. He was introduced to an entirely new audience, just because he provided value to them. People offered to take him out for beers and dinner to thank him.

This wasn't because he was the greatest writer on the planet. It was because of his blog posts. Once people received incredible value from those posts, they gleefully checked out his books and loved them. It didn't start out that way, though. It started out with him giving back without ever asking for anything in return.

This next bit is a tough pill to swallow.

You have to provide value without ever expecting anything in return. You can't keep score. You can't help somebody and then hold it over their head—you have to help without expectation of payback. That seems antithetical for success, right? I mean, how can you make a profit by helping people without monetary gain?

Well, it is difficult, but it's also incredibly powerful, because it sets you apart from everybody else. Nobody has a "value first" mentality. Everybody has a "buy first" mentality. If you can provide value first, you shake up the norm and set yourself apart from the crowd. This is a great way to stand out from the crowd which, as we talked about earlier, is important to creating your brand and gaining an audience.

Additionally, with a "value first" mentality, you will build massive goodwill in the community you want to serve and rapidly work the right people through your funnel. As a result, those people who are your ideal customer will buy from you more quickly, more often, and increase their lifetime customer value, because you provide immense value to their lives.

If you can focus on this idea of service, you will more easily make the transition from "buy first" to "value first," because it becomes not about wasting your time, but about moving people through your funnel. As we discussed earlier, it is just as important to find the 999 people who aren't a good fit for your audience as it is to find the one person who is going to buy from you forever.

Having a "value first" mentality is also a great way to start integrating buying triggers into your business. Providing value first builds up reciprocity, likability, and authority with your audience, which are three of the six key buying triggers we talked about earlier.

If you continue providing value through blogs and social media, your ideal clients will come back to you again and again, reaffirming commitment to your brand. Also, when you provide valuable advice, your customers share it with others, providing social proof to their friends so that more of your ideal clients find your work. Through providing value first, you've now hit five of those six buying triggers without even offering a product. Then, when you offer a product, you can throw in scarcity and hit all six.

Most people fear that giving away their best information will somehow diminish its value, but incredibly successful creatives like Amanda Palmer and Tim Ferris have found the opposite to be true. The more they give, the more they get in return.

Providing value is the key to finding an audience loyal to you through thick and thin, instead of being distracted by the next shiny thing that comes along. If you can develop a value first mentality now, it will serve you well in the long road of audience building that lies ahead.

TURNING A COLD PROSPECT INTO A WARM LEAD

Cold prospects don't buy products. A cold prospect is a person you just met who doesn't know you from Adam. They don't know your brand, they don't know what you offer, and they have no interest in buying what you have to sell…yet.

Cold prospects have no affinity for your product. Until you met, they had no idea who you were as a creative. That doesn't stop most creatives from seeing this initial meeting as a chance to sell their product. Of course, these efforts are a miserable failure since cold prospects don't buy products.

This makes complete sense when you think about it in your own life, doesn't it? I mean, how often do you go from discovering a new product to buying it on the same day? It doesn't happen very often in my own life.

I usually have to sit on a product for days, if not weeks, before I buy something. I need to groove on the cost and the value. I have to research the company and make sure it aligns with my values. I have to determine that the product won't turn to dust in my hands after use. My money is precious to me. I worked hard for it and want to make sure I give it to worthy people.

This is how most people see buying products, and it's why they generally buy from brands they know. When I need a hammer, I go to Home Depot because they are a brand I know. I'm not a cold prospect for them. I'm in their warm lead audience.

Warm audiences are full of people who know and trust your brand; they are the people working their way through the inside of your funnel. They gain value from what you do and are convinced your brand offers quality products. To build the most engaged audience, we need to turn as many people from cold prospects into warm leads as possible.

How do we do that? There are a couple of ways we can build devoted, warm leads from cold prospects. None of them involve shouting "buy my product" at somebody until they open their wallet.

Social media – The easiest and cheapest way to build a warm audience is through engaging with them on social media and sharing valuable content consistently. The more consistent value you can provide into a person's life by linking to interesting articles and engaging with their profiles, the more likability and authority you build with them.

It's important to post things relevant to your ideal client avatar that will drastically improve their lives, but it's even more important to be consistent over a long period of time. People value dependability. They want to know you aren't going away tomorrow before they trust you in the long run.

Mailing list – The most profitable way to turn a cold prospect into a warm lead is through creating a mailing list. When somebody gives you their email, they are allowing you into the place online they hold most dear—their inbox.

If you feed people incredibly valuable information through a newsletter, your cold audience will quickly warm up and become receptive to buying your product. This newsletter is not a list of coupons every week. It's a thoughtful piece that provides value to your audience, just like you do on social media. Creating a newsletter and delivering consistent value will make you stand out from the noise that bombards your prospects on social media every minute of every day.

Website – Your website—and its accompanying blog—is a great way to build empathy between your brand and your ideal customer. If you speak in a language your customer understands and deliver your content in a way that provides value in their lives, then customers will quickly build trust in your company. That trust equates to more warm leads and eventually into more sales.

Out of all these strategies, websites require the most work up front, the largest investment of money, and the longest amount of time to pay dividends. That's because website traffic comes from search rankings and search engines rank you for relevancy on any given topic based on traffic and clicks, among other factors. Website traffic takes time, unless you have a massive marketing budget.

You can expect your website to take six to twelve months before it starts paying off with organic traffic from search engines, but once you are ranked on the first page of search engines, that traffic keeps coming to you in perpetuity.

You can help these rankings grow quickly by consistently sharing your blog posts on social media to help drive traffic to your site. The larger your audience grows, the more traffic you will be able to generate to your site and the higher search engines will rank you.

In-person events – Whether it's speaking engagements, conventions, or even flea markets, in-person events are the quickest way to turn cold prospects into warm leads. Even though these events are expensive and time consuming, you immediately get in front of your ideal client over and over again right at the moment they are primed to buy.

The quickest way to get a prospect to like and trust you is to shake their hand and make eye contact. Getting somebody to like and trust you are two key parts of your sales funnel, and it's how we turn somebody from a cold prospect into a warm lead. Therefore, if you can shake two hundred hands at any given event, you have just moved two hundred people from cold prospects into warm leads.

If you are in the right kind of industry, phone sales and direct mail can also be effective, but I'm going to skip over their strategies for the purposes of this discussion since they are more advanced, costly, and time-intensive techniques that yield very low returns unless you already have a massive audience.

Whichever of the above strategies you employ, none of them work in a vacuum. They are interconnected pieces of the same whole. The most important part of turning a cold prospect into a warm lead is that you are meeting people now in order to turn them into sales down the road. Some people will be ready to buy immediately, but most won't warm up until much later. They need to see you, hear you, and listen to you over and over again—and over a long period of time—to build the kind of empathy necessary to buy your product.

STEAL YOUR IDEAL AUDIENCE

If you are not comfortable with the murky, gray areas of audience building, move on to the next chapter right now. This is one of the most powerful audience-building strategies around, but it's also frowned upon by every platform's terms of service.

I'll give you one more sentence to leave, okay?

Cool. Everybody who's still reading must be okay diving into the murky waters of audience building. I'm going to give you a step-by-step guide to finding the perfect people for your audience and making them part of your audience.

I call this strategy "stealing your ideal audience."

It doesn't give you as engaged a fan base as people who come of their own accord, but waiting for them could take forever and a day, and who has money to pay for tons of ads to build an audience quicker than that? Not me, that's for sure.

This strategy can build your profile by thousands of followers in a matter of weeks and costs nothing but your time. Note, this strategy works best on Twitter and Instagram, but it does work with other platforms, as well.

Step 1: Find influencers that are a perfect fit.

We first need to find the audience that would be most interested in what you have to say. Luckily, there are influencers who have spent millions building their brand into a finely honed tool that drives their ideal audience to them.

Your job, then, is to find the perfect influencer to fit your needs. If you have been following along, you should already have a list of influencers who speak to your ideal audience. Now, it's time to make that list work for you.

If you skipped over that section, influencers are celebrities and thought leaders who do exactly what you are doing in the way you want to do it. For example, Tim Burton is a huge celebrity I use to build my audience. Bryan K. Vaughn is another; Stephen King is a third. These are people who speak to my ideal audience. They have built an online and in-person marketing strategy to attract the right people.

Because they have spent years attracting the right people, you can assume their audience is going to be very interested in what you are doing as well, since you are doing similar things.

Step 2: Research where your influencers are strongest.

Now, we need to find the platforms where your influencer is strongest. If their biggest audiences are on Tumblr, Pinterest, and Twitter, those should be the cornerstones of your audience building strategy, too.

During your research, you want to take note of when they post, what they post, and how often they post. Also, consider what sorts of information gets the most engagement from their followers. Use all of this data to determine the best types of content to share with your ideal audience.

Step 3: Build your own social media profiles on those same platforms.

Once you have your market research done, it's time to build out your social media profiles on the same platforms where your influencers are the strongest.

When building your social media profiles, it's important to make several dozen posts before you even consider finding an audience. These posts should provide your ideal audience with relevant information so they want to engage with you. These posts must show you are a likeminded person who enjoys the same things as your ideal audience.

You can use sites like Buzzsumo to find the biggest stories in any given topic, or you can build a list of the topics your influencers previously covered and repost those instead. I recommend a combination of both strategies working in tandem. Don't forget to take note of any hashtags your influencer used, as many people search those to find engaging conversations.

Whichever way you choose to find your content, this step is about relevancy and consistency. You can't put up twenty posts and then stop. You have to keep feeding that content out to your audience on a regular basis or they will abandon you.

Additionally—and this will be controversial—you should strongly consider buying a thousand followers upfront if you are using Twitter, Instagram, or any other platforms where this is an option. Nobody wants to follow a person who has no followers.

Step 4: Start building your following.

Now that you have profiles on the right social media accounts and you've constructed your profile to entice the right readership, it's time to start building that following.

This is where we wade neck deep into the murky waters of audience building.

The next step is to follow everybody who follows your influencers. Statistically, somewhere between 10–15 percent of people will follow you back. Since you have, hopefully, bought those thousand followers and are posting interesting stuff that speaks to your ideal audience, you should be on the high end of that statistic.

You can also search for relevant conversations through hashtags and then follow people who use those hashtags. Since their interests align with yours, there is a very good chance they are in your ideal audience.

Most social media platforms have a rule that prevents you from following more than 150 percent of your follower count. That means if you have one thousand followers, you can only follow fifteen hundred people before you can no longer continue and have to unfollow people.

This is one reason why that base of one thousand followers is so nice to have—it allows you to follow more people than you normally would.

Step 5: Lather, Rinse, Repeat.

Once you hit your platform's follow cap, unfollow people who haven't followed you back. Then, repeat the process again, and again, and again, for as long as you want, as many times as you want, until you are satisfied.

You can use different influencers or the same ones. You can switch up hashtags, too. At certain times of the year, different hashtags will be popular, so make sure to pay attention to relevant hashtags when you are following people.

Make note, if you follow people too quickly, the platforms will catch on and ban you, so be sure not to go too fast. You can use programs like Tweetbuzz and Instagress to automate this process. They cost money, but it's easier than the headache of following and unfollowing people all day every day.

There is one more strategy that I want to include here; I call it daisy chaining. It's an amazing way to build the quality of your Facebook and LinkedIn profiles, but it means going eyeball deep into the murky waters.

Ready? Then, here we go.

When somebody looks at their friend request list, they typically only look for two things—how many mutual contacts you have in common and whether you work in the same industry. If you can meet that criteria, then they will generally approve you.

The reasoning for this is that successful creatives meet hundreds, if not thousands, of people a month. They just can't keep all of them straight. Therefore, you can short circuit their social media filter if you can just get enough mutual friends in common.

To do this on Facebook, go to your suggested friends and add every person that has even a tangential relationship with your favorite influencers and with whom you share at least twenty to thirty mutual friends. You can perform the same action on LinkedIn by searching through your mutual connections. Using the statistics from above, we can assume 10–15 percent of those people will friend you back.

Keep repeating that process until you have dozens upon dozens of mutual connections with the key influencers in your industry. Once you have at least one hundred mutual connections, you can comfortably friend request an influencer and reasonably expect they will accept you, even if you have never met in person. It's an underhanded strategy, for sure, but it also works incredibly well.

If you utilize this strategy, don't be a chump and ask for favors, or portfolio reviews, or jobs of any kind. Just be a cool person. This is about making friends and providing value. If you do cool stuff, people will take notice.

Both of these strategies are so deep into the murky water you can't see the shore line; however, they are also really effective. You can make your own judgment on whether they are right for you. What you cannot deny is that they are incredibly effective.

GET A WEBSITE ALREADY

If there's one thing I hate, it's terrible websites. I hate websites that aren't responsive and look like they were thrown together by a toddler. They make creatives look bad and I cringe at them. It doesn't matter how awesome a company's product—if it's hosted on a crappy website, they've lost my business.

The only thing I hate more than bad website design is no website at all. At least a bad website means you are in the game. You made an effort, even if it was pathetic. If you don't have a website, you might as well not even exist as a company.

Even a crappy website is getting some benefit of SEO and brand building. It's not a great benefit, but it's a benefit. You can always change the design of a website, too, and make a crappy looking website look amazing, thus moving a bad website design to a great website design while still getting all the benefit of the juicy SEO from your crappy site.

Let's take a step back. What is SEO?

Search Engine Optimization, or SEO for short, is the process of trying to reach the top of search engine rankings. It involves a complicated algorithm including clicks, backlinks, overall traffic, and hundreds of other factors that are too complicated to worry about for our purposes.

What is important to note is that SEO is one of the most important aspects of building an online brand, and it takes a long time to work. Ranking on search engines takes roughly six to twelve months to start working and ranking is very important.

Once you start ranking, organic traffic funnels into your site like magic. Organic traffic means people type a query into a search engine, your website pops up, and they click on it. It's a beautiful thing when it starts working, because it's essentially free marketing. No social outreach or advertising necessary.

Everybody benefits from SEO to some degree, except for people that don't have a website. If you don't have a website, then search engines can't find you and you will never get the benefit of this free audience-building channel.

It's sort of like the housing market. Getting into the housing market by purchasing a starter house is better than not getting into it at all, even if your house is a piece of junk.

If you are in the housing market, then your home value increases with the market. You can only move to an equally priced house in a similar neighborhood, but it's better than being on the outside of the market. When the prices rise, the person without a house might not even be able to afford your piece of garbage starter house.

I'm confronted all the time with people who tell me, "I'm launching a product in six months, so we'll launch our website around that time."

It makes me cringe.

Starting a website needs to happen at least six to twelve months before you launch your product. For one thing, you need a massive amount of time to build an audience, and your website is ground zero for that.

More importantly, if you wait until your product launches, it will take six to twelve months for search engines to start ranking you. That's up to a year without search results having any bearing on your product sales.

I get why people wait, though. Most people don't set up a website, because they are intimidated by WordPress. With good reason, by the way. WordPress is incredibly complicated to use. I use it for many of my websites, and it's a nightmare to figure out.

Luckily, you never have to use WordPress!

There are plenty of sites that use What You See Is What You Get (WYSIWYG) editors. These editors are easier to use than Photoshop. Sites like Squarespace, Wix, and Weebly allow you to build a beautiful site without the headache of WordPress. If you know a little bit of graphic design, you can make a website beautiful, and a beautiful website builds authority with your audience.

A website is critical for audience building. It acts as home base for your audience. It's a place where they can always go and engage with your brand. They can read your content. They can join your mailing list. They can order your products. Whenever they want to connect with your brand, your website gives them a place to do so. If you only use Tumblr, or Twitter, or Facebook for your base of operations, then it's like leaving your audience homeless.

There is an even bigger problem with relying on a platform like Facebook to anchor your audience. At any time, they can change their algorithm and reduce who can see your posts. Your entire business could take a dive through no fault of your own.

This happened to millions of brands when Facebook changed their algorithm so that almost nobody saw their posts unless they paid for advertising. Twitter created a similar scare when they changed their algorithm to show the most relevant posts instead of the newest ones.

This never happens with your website. On your site, you control everything. The only person who can change who sees specific content is you. The only person who makes changes to the code is you.

You control the horizontal and the vertical.

This allows you to make a cohesive and consistent brand. It also means you can add things like a mailing list, Google Analytics, and other key features that will help your audience stay inside your ecosystem as long as possible, and allow you to touch them more easily should they leave.

If you have put off building a website, it's time to take the plunge. If you aren't comfortable with HTML or even WordPress, there are plenty of WYSIWYG editors out there that can give you the internet presence you need to build your career.

Even a crappy site is better than no site at all, if just barely. A website is something you can create yourself with very little time and effort. Any of the WYSIWYG editors take at most a couple days to set up and cost $100-$200 per year.

If they are too complicated for you, then hire a web designer to set up your site. However, you must have a website. It is an essential ingredient to your success. It's the bedrock foundation for everything else you do online.

WHAT IF YOU DON'T HAVE A PRODUCT YET?

Audience building needs to begin well before there is ever a product to sell. In fact, your product will probably be little more than a glimmer in your mind when it's time to set up a website and start building out your SEO.

A quality marketing push needs six to twelve months of lead time to build appropriate buzz before a product hits market. Without a properly motivated audience, your product will be dead in the water before you ever release it. This prompts the obvious question, "How do you build an audience if you won't have a product for a year?"

Well, I'll tell you.

Let's say you want to create a series of paintings about famous American haunted houses. You want to make them available on your website as prints, an art book, and a calendar. The only problem is that it will take a year to complete and you haven't told anybody about your plans.

How do you create an excited audience for your haunted house paintings if you don't even have an inkling of a glimmer of an audience yet?

Step 1: Set up a website with the domain for your print series. Let's say it's hauntedmansionsofamerica.com. This site will house your store, your blog, and everything a person needs to know in order to buy your product.

Step 2: Search the internet for articles, pictures, and general information on haunted mansions. You aren't going to post about them yet. Right now, you are simply building a cache of information about haunted mansions, including people who have studied them, ghost hunters who have investigated them, owners of haunted properties, and other information that somebody who likes haunted mansions wants to know.

Step 3: Start sharing haunted mansion information on social media, in forums, and in Facebook groups related to haunted mansions. You aren't selling anything right now. You are only adding value to your audience's lives, which builds up their trust. You haven't asked anybody to even go to your website yet. Meanwhile, you are contacting the owners of these haunted mansions, ghost hunters, and people who work in that arena, and setting up interviews for your own blog.

Step 4: Start compiling the information you gathered into what are called epic blog posts. Epic blog posts are 2,500 word (or more) posts that provide a massive amount of information on a very specific topic. For instance, "Every Haunted House in New England (and what ghosts to expect inside each one)," or "Everything You Need to Know Before You Start Hunting Ghosts in the Deep South," or "The 50 Scariest Things People Who've Encountered Ghosts Have Ever Said." These epic blog posts form the bedrock of your SEO strategy. You should plan on sharing these on a consistent basis, because they will be timeless ways to provide value to your audience.

Your goal should be to write five or six of these within the first forty-five days of launching your blog. Pepper these posts with your own sketches to spruce up the content and get people excited about your paintings. Never forget: The end goal is to sell your work.

Step 5: Create a haunted mansion mailing list people can sign up for on your site. Make sure to fill every newsletter with valuable content catered to people who love haunted mansions. Spice up your newsletters with your own paintings to give it a graphic pop and keep people excited about your work.

Step 6: Once you release your epic blog post, you want to start mixing in interviews with haunted mansion owners, accounts of ghost sightings, and interviews with ghost hunters into your blog. This is a great way to build up authority with people who can help make your launch a success. Perhaps the owners would be willing to stock an exclusive print in their gift shop, or a ghost hunter would shout out your art book on their social media accounts. Now, you are providing value to your audience, building your authority, and making connections that can help jettison your launch toward success.

You have moved from just sharing content on forums to creating original content exclusive to your brand. This makes you a destination site for everybody who wants to know more about haunted mansions. Since these people love haunted mansions, what do you think the chances are they want an art print, or an art book, from somebody who has proven they are an expert in the field? Pretty darn good.

Step 7: By now we have five of the six buying triggers whipping your ideal audience into a fervor. You've built massive commitment, likability, social proof, reciprocity, and authority with the exact people who should love your work most.

It's time to start talking openly about your project. This is not about pitching. It's about offering insights into your process, showing in-progress pages, images, getting feedback, and offering behind-the-scenes content. If you do this right, people will clamor to order your artwork when it becomes available.

Step 8: Start preorders for your product. Offer a slight discount for the first people to order. This hits upon the scarcity trigger. Now, you've delivered on all six triggers. While handling preorders, continue offering valuable content about haunted mansions.

Step 9: Launch your project into the world with masses of people who love what you do!

All of this takes time. This is a year of work boiled down into a couple of pages. It's not easy; it's not quick. You will get frustrated. You will have false starts and stops. You will do things wrong. Your growth will stall for no discernable reason multiple times. You'll want to rip out all your hair. That's okay. Even the best fail at this constantly, but they don't stop. They never stop.

The key is to keep going. If you work toward this blueprint, you'll be able to build a rabid audience desperate for what you have to offer them.

It just takes time. There's no shortcut to that.

THE SECRET TO BUILDING A MEMORABLE BRAND

There are millions of flashy logos and interesting-looking websites floating around the internet, but they are almost always hollow and unmemorable. I want to love them, but they leave me asking the same two questions: "What are you trying to say here?" and "Who are you trying to say it to?"

These are the two basic questions you must ask when building a brand, and too often they are often skipped over in favor of a flashy logo that screams nothing into the void but "Look at me, I'm pretty!"

This is antithetical to a brand's purpose. The purpose of a brand is to stand above the void and scream, "Look at me. I'm perfect for you!" It may be fun to have a cool logo, but flashy design doesn't serve the purpose of building a brand identity.

The purpose of a brand is to speak for you when you aren't there to speak for yourself. It's a reflection of you in the eyes of your ideal customers. Its job is to provide a beacon for your audience in the endless, hyper-connected fog in which we live.

Look at a company like Apple. Steve Jobs couldn't speak to every human being on the planet. He was a busy guy. Even if he could, he wouldn't be able reach out again and again over the course of decades. He needed something that could repeatedly speak for him in the minds of the populace. Enter the Apple brand, possibly the greatest brand in the history of the world.

In Apple's advertising, logo, and design aesthetic, Jobs had to convey exactly what people could expect from his products without saying a single word to them. He had to create a brand so powerful that his perfect audience would rise up from the endless void and hone in on his company.

This is what the right brand can do for your company. It can turn your audience building inside out and lead the right people to your door.

If you do it correctly, of course.

Generally, creatives go about building a brand too early in their company's life cycle. I know it's tough to hold off on branding since we have artistic energy brimming from every orifice, but a memorable brand isn't about artistic talent.

It's about emotional connection with your audience.

Look at the "Life is Good" logo. There's almost no artistic talent needed to draw that stick figure, and yet it resonated with people so deeply they were able to build a company that's held up for decades.

Most creatives think a good company starts with a solid brand, but in reality the branding should be the last thing that comes about in the life cycle of a company. Until you have pinpointed your ideal customer avatar and have a complete product line aimed at them, it's useless to think about creating a brand that could change drastically with every product launch.

To fully understand your brand, you must be able to say, "This is what my company stands for," "this is who I build my products for," and "this is what I'm trying to say." This only comes with time, market research, and speaking extensively to your perfect customers.

For Wannabe Press, our history with Kickstarter made a green and yellow color scheme very appealing to me. Not only does the green stand out on marketing materials, but the coloring harkens back to our roots with grassroots fundraising.

We modeled our rebellious bee mascot off of *Invader Zim*, a children's cartoon created by Jhonen Vasquez. He was a huge influence on me and an even bigger influence on my audience. Once we figured that out, it was a no brainer to use *Invader Zim* as the basis for our logo. We filled her with attitude, because that rebellious spirit embodied everything we knew about our ideal customers.

We didn't start with our mascot, though. We only designed it after years of building our audience. It was borne out of seeing how people reacted to our products. It came from watching who bought our books again and again. It was a reflection of what we saw in the people who liked our products. We weren't trying to stuff a mascot down our audience's throats. We saw what they responded to and made something that spoke to them.

That's the true secret to building a memorable brand. You build it as you go until it reflects your ideal client perfectly. They tell you exactly what they want, and then you mirror it back to them. Once you can do that, your brand will stick out like a beacon in the endless void.

THE MAILING LIST

We are programmed to think of newsletters as spam and mailing lists as evil. They don't have to be spam, though, and they certainly aren't evil. If you set it up right, a mailing list is the most effective form of online marketing in existence for building empathy and trust with your customers.

The truth is that a mailing list is only annoying if the information is unwanted. When I think about annoying emails, I think about Target. They send me so many emails filled with promotions and coupons. I hate those! I'm not going to Target just to save thirty-five cents on a bucket of toilet paper!

But that's just me. Not everybody feels that way.

There are lots of people who love Target. There are people who really, really want to hear what Target has to say. They shop at Target every week. They need toilet paper and are always looking for a bargain. For those people, Target isn't sending junk. They are sending incredibly valuable information.

That's how we must look at our mailing list.

It's not about spamming people. It's about offering incredible value to the people who want to be touched by your message. Customers love to be touched by the brands they love. If you consistently provide new and interesting information, your ideal customers will gobble it up.

This won't be everybody on your list, or even most people who sign up. Many people who sign up to your mailing list will think it's spam. They will unsubscribe. Good! I have a 31 percent unsubscribe rate on my emails and I love it.

You can't focus on the people who don't want your message. You don't even want them on your list thinking your information is spam. That devalues what you have to say.

You need to focus on the people who will love your message. For those people, your email can be a bright spot in their day. They may be looking forward to your email with great anticipation.

Across the board, successful marketers swear by mailing lists. They cite email as the most effective way to grow their brand and build their revenue. Even if you feel icky about setting up a mailing list, without one you are leaving money on the table.

I really don't want you to leave money on the table, so I'm still going to show you the key elements to setting up a successful mailing list. This won't be about what kind of stuff to send. We talked about that before. These are the functional elements you need to get your newsletter up and running.

A mailing list service – To provide a newsletter, you need to sign up for a service that sends and stores emails. The easiest is MailChimp. It gives you two thousand emails for free. Once you get into the paid functionality it is very expensive. Constant Contact and Aweber are the two other massive brands in the email marketing space. They all have similar pricing and functionality.

I don't use any of them. I switched to Sendinblue, which is cheaper and has more functionality than any of the big boys, even though it is more complicated to use.

There are dozens of other sites which can perform this functionality for you, so don't send emails from your Gmail account.

A free offer – A free offer gets people from searching through your website to making a commitment to your brand. They receive a piece of valuable information in exchange for their email address. This small affirmation is the first step to priming the customer to buy from you. They have acknowledged that your information is worth something, even if it's only their email address.

This free offer should represent the kinds of products or services you sell. Its goal is to immediately provide incredible value on the first email, so they can start building likability and reciprocity with your company.

If you are an author, give away an eBook for free to prove you can write. If you are an artist, give a wallpaper so people see your art every time they shut down a program. If you are selling your services, provide a cheat sheet which can help your clients get over a hurdle in their own life. These are just a couple of suggestions. There are thousands of free offers that could work for your company.

A website widget – Online mailing list subscribers come into your pipelines through your website. You need to make it easy for them to sign up by adding a signup form to your site. I recommend Sumome as they have multiple options to test conversions. I use their welcome mat and exit intent pop-up with great success.

An autoresponder sequence – An autoresponder, or indoctrination sequence, is an automated series of emails your subscribers start receiving after they sign up for your email list. These emails are staggered throughout several days or weeks so that people unfamiliar with your brand learn who you are and what you do.

Remember, people sign up for your list because of a free offer. They have no clue what you do or why your mailing list is special. An autoresponder sequence hits them in the feels, helps them get emotionally connected to you, and builds brand awareness with your ideal customers.

An autoresponder sequence replaces the function of sending five to ten personal emails to every new subscriber. Who has time for that? Not me. That's for sure. This is the main reason I chose Sendinblue, because the autoresponder sequence was a free add on to a very cheap plan, as opposed to MailChimp which charged an incredible markup to use this feature.

An offline signup application – I get most of my email subscribers at live events. Since conventions tend to have terrible reception, it's important to have a way to take email subscriptions offline. There are multiple apps for this, but my favorite is MailChimp Subscribe. It's free and works on any tablet, even if you don't have an internet connection.

The biggest hurdle I run into when convincing somebody to start a mailing list is the argument that they have nothing to say. Luckily, if you've been following along, you won't have that problem. All you have to do is pull from your list of influencers, or head on over to Buzzsumo, and use that as the base of your emails.

One of the best at using this technique is Tim Ferris. Tim built the "Four-Hour Workweek" brand into an international phenomenon, but his weekly newsletter isn't about his work. It's called "5 bullet Fridays." It's five articles, gadgets, or other things that Tim found interesting in his pursuits throughout the week.

His method is so easy and simple that anybody can do it.

You don't need to offer your mailing list new products or services every week. You don't need to provide discount codes. You just need to provide incredibly valuable information to your audience consistently, and they will be committed to your brand.

The more value you give, the more authority you build and the more they will grow to like and trust you. Because you significantly improve their lives, your subscribers will want to return the favor when it comes time to buy your product.

ADVERTISING YOUR PRODUCTS

Advertising is a piece of your overall marketing campaign, but it's a different beast entirely from everything we've talked about so far. While marketing is mostly a time commitment, you can't advertise without money.

Your goal with advertising is to spend a dollar and make two dollars in sales. At the very least, you want to spend one dollar and get one dollar out. Too often, people spend a dollar and get twenty-five cents back, or even less. If you do that, then you're funneling a massive amount of money into a campaign and getting nothing in return. It's a travesty when that happens.

But there has to be something to advertising, right? I mean McDonald's and Starbucks spend billions of dollars on it every year. They aren't going to do that without getting a return. And every other post on Facebook is for somebody pitching some sort of product, isn't it? So, somebody's making money on ads, aren't they?

The short answer is yes.

Nobody is going to keep spending money on something that loses them money, least of all a Fortune 500 company. If advertising didn't work, companies wouldn't do it. So, what is it people do wrong when it comes to advertising?

They start too early, for one. Before you start advertising, you must know your target market down pat and have a fully realized ideal customer avatar. Your avatar needs to translate successfully into proven clients you can rely on consistently.

Your funnel also needs to be rock solid. You must know how many people have to go into the top of it to make money come out the bottom. Everything you have done up to this point—honing your ideal customer avatar and perfecting your funnel—pays off in spades with advertising. This is where you scale all that work into a lucrative business.

Up until this point, you've watched your ideal client trickle through your funnel slowly over time. You've seen the wording they like and what they hate. You've noticed which links they click and which they don't care about at all. You have a good sense not just who your client is, but also what buying triggers they respond to best.

This information becomes critical when you are building an advertising campaign. With advertising, you are pushing a massive amount of people through your funnel. If they don't like what you have to say, they'll abandon you before buying. If you don't have this laid out perfectly, advertising isn't for you…yet.

The second mistake people make with advertising is treating every potential customer the same way. As we talked about earlier, there are two types of people in your audience—cold prospects and warm leads.

People screw up on advertising because we tend to treat everybody like a warm lead. Warm leads already know you. Some of them even like and trust you. They understand your brand and believe in it. Cold prospects have none of that empathy built up for your company. They don't know you from Adam.

Unless you are launching a product to your existing network, most ads are built to target cold prospects and not warm leads. You can send a warm lead directly to a product offer, but you can't do that with a cold prospect.

I see this all the time with Kickstarter campaigns. I'll be fed an ad from somebody I don't know and sent directly to their campaign page. I don't know them. I don't like them. I don't trust them. So, I'm never going to buy from that person even if their campaign is awesome. Consequently, they've just wasted sixty cents because they treated me like a warm lead even though I'm a cold prospect.

In advertising, you treat a cold prospect the same as if you'd just met them on the street—you need to provide value first before you ask for anything. This is so much harder with advertising than any other form of marketing, because you are paying cash *now* for the hope of making money in the future. If you aren't comfortable with that, advertising isn't for you…yet.

With a cold prospect, you must send them to a piece of content that adds incredible value to their lives and also relates to your product. It needs to resonate with your intended prospect. You can deliver this value in a webinar, a blog post, or even a guide that potential customers can download. The point of this content is to pack a powerful punch and make the prospect fervently believe they must learn more about your offer.

At the end of this piece of content, make an offer so they sign up for your mailing list. If they don't sign up, retarget them with new ads and even more valuable content until they relent. In order to retarget people, you have to set up Google Adwords and a Facebook pixel, along with retargeting pixels from any other advertising networks you use.

Once they sign up for your mailing list, you have received their commitment and they become a warm lead. Put them into your existing funnel and have them work their way down it just like everybody else.

If you've done your job right, you know exactly how many people need to go into the top of your funnel to get money out of the bottom of it. If you don't have this information, then advertising isn't right for you…yet.

Given the choice, my preference is to advertise only to warm leads. Warm leads are people who are on my mailing list or my Facebook page, or already access my website. These people know and like me, so they are much more likely to buy right away.

The problem with warm lead advertising is that you quickly exhaust your existing customer base and need more cold prospect to grow your revenue. Warm leads are not enough to sustain a business. You need cold prospects, too.

You absolutely should not do any advertising until you know your ideal client avatar precisely and are completely on top of how your funnel works. If you know those two things, then you can work backwards and determine a reasonable advertising budget. If you don't, then you'll just be wasting money.

Even if you are ready, start small and work your way up. There's no need to spend more than five dollars a day until you can prove advertising is a wise investment for your business.

GET SOME PRESS

Creatives hold up the press on a magical pedestal like gods, but they are really just people like you or me. They can't open some mystic lock on your career. They can't make it rain money on you. But that doesn't stop people from believing that a positive press writeup will send their careers into the stratosphere.

In no way, shape, or form is that how the press works. Out of a million articles, maybe one story will be picked up nationally, and it can make your career overnight. That chance is so insignificant, though, you would be better served searching for a tap-dancing shark singing at a cabaret.

That doesn't mean the press aren't useful. They have an incredibly powerful part to play in building your audience.

What the press can do is amplify your project to their audience. This exposes more people to your work. As you accumulate more press contacts, your message gets amplified more and more.

The press can also legitimize your work in the eyes of the buying public. When searches for your name return results that include in-depth interviews and positive reviews of your work, you've built your authority and social proof without lifting a finger.

Building press contacts is a long-term marketing strategy. It should not be a focus when you start your business. You are much better served in the short term by creating a solid brand, a massive audience, and an awesome lineup of products. Those are all things you can control. If you do them right, then the press will seek you out.

That's not to say you shouldn't work on this at all in the beginning of your career. It just shouldn't be your focus. You should spend no more than twenty to thirty minutes a day on finding press contacts, but like anything else, if you put a little bit of work into it over a long period of time, it can pay dividends in the end. If you want to build up your press contacts, here are six powerful strategies that work in any industry.

Target the right people. Even in the same industry, press contacts have tastes as varied as the human race itself. In music, for instance, some will be into rock, others into rap, and still others into country. Before you start sending out press releases, make sure you are targeting the right people.

This can easily be accomplished by cross-referencing press contacts with your existing list of influencers. If you type your influencer's name into a search engine and add either "article" or "review," hundreds of articles will show up. These articles all have bylines with the names of people who cover your exact type of product.

From there, you can cross-reference them on social media to make sure they still work in the press corps, and follow them to start building a relationship. Whatever you do, don't ask for a review right away. Treat them just like any other human being.

Ask for an introduction. If you have a friend who's been interviewed by a media outlet that would be perfect for your work, ask them to introduce you. The worst they can say is no. Even then, you can still email the press contact and say, "I loved the interview you conducted with my friend. If you liked their work, you'll love mine."

When you make an introduction, whether it's a cold introduction or through a friend, make sure to personalize it with why you think they would be a good fit to cover your project. Add some positive reviews of their work, too, but make it genuine. People can spot a fake, especially people who deal with hundreds a day.

Hone your press release. Reporters are overworked and inundated with crappy material. Their inbox is teeming with useless garbage. I feel so bad for them. It's no wonder they have a reputation for being jaded.

The good news is, if you can show them something awesome, they are likely to run with it. If it's print-ready, then it's a near certainty they will.

So, if you want to stand out, you need to show them an amazing product, in a well-formatted article ready for print, free of errors and accompanied by images. Help the press out and they will love you for it.

Get to live events. The quicker you can start exhibiting at live events, the quicker you will start acquiring valuable press contacts. The more you exhibit, the more you will acquire. Being behind the table is a great way to set yourself apart from other creators, not just in the eyes of the common crowd, but in the minds of the press, as well.

I can't tell you how many interviews I've done just because I was behind the table and the press passed by with their gear. My opening line for the press is either "I'm a media whore!" or "I love the press." It usually gets them to stop and chuckle if nothing else.

Engage on social media. The key to reporters knowing who you are is to engage with them in a compelling and interesting way. This doesn't mean make a grand gesture so they'll cover your product.

It means sharing their posts, replying to them in an intelligent manner, and generally being fun to be around. It's no different than developing a friendship.

When you interact with reporters like they are human beings and not meat popsicles that can help your career, you set yourself apart from everybody else who only wants something from them.

Become one of them. Every news site needs good contributors. There are more stories than any site can cover effectively. If you can write, know a lot about your field, and you're ready to review anything that comes across your desk, contact sites and start writing for them.

You won't write for every outlet you contact, but some will certainly need your help. This is a great way to build up reciprocity with press contacts while building social proof and authority with your audience. Then, when your product launches, you have grown your ideal audience by providing content and built advocacy with fellow reporters who want you to succeed.

Make sure when you contact these press outlets, you are giving them information that is both ready to print, thus free of spelling and grammar errors, and, if possible, newsworthy.

Newsworthiness means your piece is both timely and relevant to your contact's audience. Launching a new board game, for instance, may be newsworthy to you, but most people don't care about your product.

However, if you happen to be launching your product during National Board Game Day, you might be able to schedule an interview with a local news station to show them why board games are important. Success with the press is all about making your work relevant and newsworthy for their audience.

It takes a ton of work to build a solid base of press contacts. Most of your efforts will be in vain, but it's important to keep working at it little by little. Over time, those little gains add up to a solid rolodex of reporters who can help shine a light on your projects.

Whatever you do, remember to come from a value first mentality with no expectation anybody will do anything for you. Your goal is to foster a relationship that will last for decades...and that only happens with time.

THE THREE DEGREES OF SOCIAL MEDIA ENGAGEMENT

The purpose of social media is two-fold. First, it's meant to drive engagement and empathy with your brand. Social media is not about blasting out your products all the time. It's the opposite of that, actually. Think of social media like it's a cocktail party. If you wouldn't say it when you meet somebody at a cocktail party, don't say it on social media.

There is a time and a place for talking about your work, and that's when somebody asks, "What do you do?" There is a point in the flow of every conversation which will naturally lead to that question. It usually comes after you ask, "What do you do?" and give somebody the opportunity to talk about themselves. The more you can get a person to open up, the more likely they are to build a relationship with you. The deeper your connection, the more likely they are to buy from you.

The second purpose of social media is to drive people onto your website so they can read your content. That's not an easy task. People are inundated with awesome stuff all the time. To convince them your content is as important as *Buzzfeed* or *The Washington Post*, you need to stand above all the other social media noise.

We do that by creating a mini-funnel on social media utilizing the strengths of multiple platforms to grow your brand. This is very similar to your overall sales funnel, but it is hyper-targeted to reach through the void on social media and drive people to connect with your profile in a more meaningful way.

The **first degree of social media engagement** uses sites that specialize in congregating a massive volume of people. These are the platforms where influencers have the biggest network. Some examples of these are places like Pinterest, Twitter, and Instagram, along with Facebook Pages.

These sites function like a networking event. Your goal is to talk to as many people as possible to find the best fits for your product. You won't make many deep connections, but you make up in quantity what you lack in quality. You can't have a successful business without exposing yourself to new groups in this manner.

With first degree social media engagement, you allow new people to dip their toe in the water with your brand. They see that you curate interesting content and get to know you better as a person, making them want to build a connection with you.

You must start with this kind of platform to be successful. If you focus on a platform further down your funnel, you will have trouble building that initial traction and struggle to build any audience at all.

Second degree social media engagement involves people interacting with your content. Instead of curating other people's work, you become the commentator.

This kind of engagement is like meeting a potential friend for coffee. You've found somebody interesting at a networking event, and you want to get to know them more intimately—but you don't want to waste all day, either.

It's important for people to recognize your voice and see your face in order to build this kind of engagement. Humans have more connection with people they can see and hear than with the words they read, so second-tier social media engagement must involve video—there are no ifs, ands, or buts about it. If you aren't comfortable being on camera, that's okay. You can work up to this level of engagement. Remember, everything is a process.

Even though there is video involved, this kind of engagement doesn't have to look pretty. It doesn't have to be perfect. It shouldn't be long, either. You don't want to monopolize a person's life. You just want to say hello, give a bit of quality insight, and say goodbye. This shouldn't take more than a couple of minutes, max. Sites that specialize in this kind of engagement are YouTube, Facebook Live, and Snapchat.

Third degree social media engagement is about connecting deeply with your audience. This type of engagement takes a massive time commitment on the part of both you and your fans.

Think of this level of engagement like a long dinner. You aren't going to have a long dinner with just anybody, but they lead to the most meaningful interactions because you have somebody's undivided attention for a massive amount of time. In third degree social media engagement, you exchange quality for quantity. This is where the best engagement happens, but you can't build a large following at this level without engaging in first and second degree engagement, as well.

While first degree engagement only last seconds and second degree engagement is just a couple minutes long, this third degree of engagement could last up to an hour or more. Third degree social media engagement happens on sites like Blab, Periscope, and Twitch.

A social media funnel directs people to follow you online in a more personal way. The deeper they go, the more fulfilling the experience for both you and them. Not everybody in your first degree funnel will take the journey into the second and third degree levels of engagement, but those who do are more likely to buy your product and feel a personal connection with you.

If the idea of this kind of funnel overwhelms you, don't feel the need to set it up immediately. Like anything else in a creative career, this takes time to get right. Putting together even one successful platform is time consuming.

While your long-term goal should be to have this funnel set up, your short-term goal is to find the perfect first degree platform to engage your audience and build your voice. It's better to be really good at one platform than mediocre at a bunch. Nobody follows mediocrity.

PART 4

MAKING MONEY AT LIVE EVENTS

Live events are festering cesspools of wasted money for most creators. Most creatives know live shows are important for their career, but don't know how to use them to make money or to grow their brand. It ends up being a financial burden instead of a lucrative, money-making opportunity.

The good news is that it's very possible to make money and grow your brand at live shows. If you can do it right, live shows are the absolute best opportunity to quickly build and maintain a passionate audience that will buy from you.

That's the beauty of live events, but it takes incorporating much of what we've talked about previously into the live event experience. It means thinking about live events differently than you do now, and understanding how to make the live event experience work for you.

Live events are the easiest way to build an audience, as well. People are a lot nicer and more engaging in person than they are online. Since you are directly in front of customers with your wares, you can quickly turn somebody from a cold prospect into a warm lead—and even convince them to buy—in a single interaction.

The best thing about live events is that everybody who passes your table is a potential customer. They have all paid to get in and decided to walk through your area. In doing so, they have self-selected themselves as being interested in what you have to offer. Now, the trick is just convincing them you are the right vendor for their needs.

Before you read through this section, I highly recommend going back to take notes on the sales funnel, pitching, and mailing list lessons we discussed earlier. I'm not going over them again in this section, and they are critical to your success at live shows.

The most important aspect of live show success is to get in the right mindset before you walk into the door. It's critical that you are prepared to deal with people for ten hours a day for the entire length of the show. Live events will drain you. You need to have a full battery before you walk into the convention center, and you will need time to recharge that battery before the following day.

Everybody has different tricks when it comes to getting in the right mindset. It could mean psyching yourself up in a car for thirty minutes, finding an anchor point with people you know, or picturing everybody naked. Whatever your secret, you need to find the right headspace in order to be successful. All the tactics in the world won't work unless you are mentally ready to employ them.

I know you will want to curl up in a ball and hide after your first unsuccessful pitch, but you have to keep going. Just remember, home is just a few hours away—however, you paid a lot of money to be at the show, and you need to make the most out of it. It's way better to head home with a big wad of cash in your pocket than to have nothing but a hoarse voice to show for your effort.

MAKE IT AN EXPERIENCE

People go to shows to have fun. They could be sitting at home eating bonbons, but instead they chose to leave their house and come to your event. Every single person at your event has overcome a tremendous amount of laziness just to be there. They could be watching a movie, doing ceramics, eating at a nice restaurant, or engaging in any number of activities, but instead they have chosen to spend their time with you.

As such, if we want to be successful, then we must craft an experience that engages our ideal customer. The more we design our booths to maximize the enjoyment of the fans, the more successful we will be exhibiting at live events. If people come up to you, have a good experience, and enjoy your products, they will be more likely to buy what you have to offer.

People want to buy things. We are a consumerist society. The people at the shows are your perfect customers, because in walking through the door, they've already been primed to buy even if they don't want to buy your stuff, per se.

They are looking for something that connects them emotionally with the show itself. Whether it is a book, a CD, a movie, or a necklace, people want to look at the stuff they buy and positively remember the experience of being at the show.

After all, customers can buy necklaces anywhere, usually for cheaper than you are making them. They can type in a search on Amazon and find a charm just like yours at half the price. But it's not about that for customers at live events. It's about emotional connection.

Have you ever been on vacation? Every souvenir is super overpriced, no matter if it's wine, jewelry, or ugly hats. Logically, you are crazy to buy any souvenirs on vacation, because they jack up the prices. Yet, we all do it.

Why?

It's because we connect those overpriced trinkets to a happy experience. The better the experience, the more our connection grows and the more that ugly hat is worth. The same is true with live events. The reason customers buy from you is because they made an emotional connection they will remember forever.

They can go home and give their daughter a gift from the show. They can read your book and remember the positive experience of meeting you. They can hang your print and relive memories of the awesome time they had for the rest of their lives.

When planning your booth, it's important to think about the overall experience of the customer. This isn't just about your persona, either. Yes, you need to be engaging. You need to smile, laugh, and put your product in somebody's hand. Your pitch needs to be perfect. You need to know the exact triggers to pull to get somebody to buy.

But it doesn't end there.

You need to cater your table in every way to attract your perfect customer. This means setting up your table so it stands out, using bright colors to draw the eye, and implementing signage that drives traffic. It means creating eye-catching products and making con exclusives so that people connect your brand with the positive emotional experience of the convention itself. It means offering your customers something they can't get anywhere else.

Your job is to create an experience so enticing for your ideal customer that they will seek you out at every show they attend, because you have crafted an experience they love. This takes a little while to get right, which is all the more reason you need to get started right away.

When Wannabe Press first started, we didn't have our green banner or mascot. We didn't give away free prints or buttons at shows. We waited until we knew our customer, knew what they wanted, and then we pounced.

However, we didn't delay in starting to craft the perfect experience; we began work on that immediately. We went to our first con and offered free crappy drawings so that people saw our personality and got a con exclusive. We laughed and smiled. We pitched our books, yes, but we also left people with a positive experience they could treasure forever. People still come up and ask about our crappy drawings even today.

The experience you provide will improve over time as you become more comfortable at live shows and better understand your customer, but it's important to start crafting the experience before you even start exhibiting so every customer has the best chance of falling in love with your brand at first sight.

WHAT IS YOUR UNFAIR ADVANTAGE?

I've heard writers complain about not being able to sell at shows ever since I started attending them oh so many years ago. Writers can't draw, so there is no way for them to sell originals, prints, or commissions—which is what people want at shows, right?

If that's true, then why do artists complain about not having books on their table? If people only wanted art, then all artists should kill it at every show, shouldn't they?

And what about publishers? They didn't even create the books. They just stamp their logo on other people's creations, don't they? How can they succeed? Nobody at shows wants to buy a book unless the creator of the book is sitting there and signing, right?

If you've ever thought any of these questions, you have properly diagnosed a major issue in making money at conventions, which is that artists, writers, and publishers must operate differently to succeed.

Writers, artists, and publishers all have different unfair advantages at shows. An unfair advantage is what allows you to succeed in any given situation. It is something that cannot be copied or replicated by others. In order to sell at live shows, it's important to focus on your specific unfair advantage.

The unfair advantage of an artist is that they have a visceral, immediate connection to their audience. An artist can sell prints, art books, originals, and commissions at shows. They are an immediate draw for customers. We are visual creatures and visual art speaks for itself. For writers, people need to invest in the story, but for artists everything they need to connect with their audience is front and center.

However, an artist is stuck working on a couple projects at a time. The work of an artist takes longer than the work of a writer. An amazingly fast artist can finish one page a day from beginning to end, which means the maximum output of the artist is 365 pages a year. Since the average graphic novel is 100-150 pages, that means an artist can create a maximum of three graphic novels a year.

Even though that is a ton of completed work, it pales in comparison to the writer. The writer's unfair advantage is they can create a massive amount of work, in different mediums, at the same time. While the artist is stuck in visual mediums, a writer can expand into prose, or even write movies and television.

While it takes an artist many months to draw a book, a writer can finish a five-issue graphic novel in a couple weeks, max. A prolific writer can finish an issue a day, which means a prolific writer can produce 365 issues in a given year. If the average graphic novel is five or six issues, the writer can crank out sixty to seventy graphic novels a year. That's twenty times more than the artist.

If a potential customer doesn't like one visual style, a writer can present a book with a different visual style and hope to make a sale. An artist is limited by their personal visual range, but a writer can work with many different artists of varying styles.

Additionally, if somebody does not like comic books, a writer can show novels or even movie scripts. If a writer can focus on the variety of their table, they can sell as much as an artist or even more. If writers focus on mimicking the unfair advantage of an artist, they will never be able to compete.

I often see writers with only one book on their table, wondering why they aren't making the same types of sales as an artist. But their lackluster sales should make complete sense given what we now know, right?

They aren't making sales because they haven't leveraged their unfair advantage. They're trying to mimic how an artist makes money even though a writer generates sales in a completely different manner. While an artist can make money at a show selling a single book along with prints and commissions, a writer needs to focus on their own unfair advantage in order to succeed.

The publisher has a different unfair advantage than both the writer and artist. A publisher's unfair advantage is the ability to put out a massive amount of books from many different creators. If a potential customer doesn't like one creator or style, they can shift gears and show them a completely different person's work.

A company like Simon & Schuster publishes over two thousand titles a year. They don't create any of those works in house. They hire out writers or acquire the rights to properties, then edit and release those books. They own the means of production and can push out a massive volume of titles. What they lose in the creation of the books they make up for in the variety of books they publish.

No matter how hard a writer or artist works, they could never finish that many works in any given year, at least not publishable ones. So, the publisher's unfair advantage is in the variety and volume of creators they have in their catalog, and their ability to leverage those creators to build their brand.

The problem is that most creators pine for the unfair advantage of somebody else. Or worse, they try to emulate the unfair advantage of another type of creative. If a writer tries to sell a single book instead of focusing on variety, then they are not utilizing their unfair advantage. With one book, a writer can never hope to make as much as an artist.

An artist, in contrast, needs to focus on their unique style and understand that their advantage lies in people committing to their art style. The more art they have on their table that is unique to them, the better chance they have of being successful. This might include a book, but it can also include originals, prints, and commissions.

For a publisher, the unfair advantage lies in having a massive amount of choice and enticing readers with the variety of creators they have available. One, two, or even ten books might not be enough to utilize that unfair advantage.

So, what is your unfair advantage?

SET UP YOUR TABLE FOR SUCCESS

Convention sales are won or lost before the first person passes your booth. They are decided before the doors even open. Whether you will make money or not is decided the moment you drag your stuff into the convention hall and set up your table.

Most tables are a hot mess, so it's no wonder nobody buys from them. There is no order. There is no flow. It's just a bunch of stuff with no direction. If artists sell prints, there is an enormous wall for people to choose with dozens of options and no guidance. Often, artists construct edifices around them so elaborate you can barely see them at all.

That's not inviting.

Don't forget, it's your job to take your customer by the hand and give them an experience. A massive print wall isn't an experience, it's a nightmarish hellscape fraught with danger and filled with too many choices.

A print wall seems great in theory, but in practice it overwhelms your clients. More importantly, it gives them no reason to connect with you. They don't have to interact. They don't have to engage. They just have to point.

The opposite is true with an artist with a closed book of prints on their table. There is nothing to draw a customer's eye. There is nothing to focus their interest. There is no reason for them to stop unless they already know your work. The advantage of a print book is that customers have to stop and open it, but you still have to get them to your table.

Luckily, there is a better way to set up your table—without any of that massive set-up or monetary commitment—that builds interest with your ideal customer while forcing them to interact with you.

I learned this method by walking the exhibit hall at dozens of cons and noticing how the successful artists differed from the mediocre ones. I found the common themes all of the big exhibitor booths had in common, and I reverse engineered them to work at my booth.

This method takes less than thirty minutes to set up, and can be scaled up to a full ten-by-ten exhibitor booth or all the way down to a three-foot table.

You need five products in total to make this table set-up work: two bestselling items on either side of your table, two niche products behind them, and a cheap or free product up front. Together, they create an alleyway from the front of the table right to you standing behind it.

The most important products on your table are the bestselling items. If you don't know your bestselling items already, take some time to show your products to people and see which ones they are most likely to buy. Don't worry if you get this wrong at first, you can always change it later.

Bestselling items usually outsell the rest of your table by a three to one margin, or more. Since these products are now the focus of your table instead of hidden around other products, your ideal client can immediately develop a connection to them. This is also great for you. Now that you are focusing on a couple of products, you can order more of them, thus increasing your profit margins.

Once you have your best-selling items locked in, it's time
to set up your two niche products. These are placed behind
your bestsellers and closer to the middle of the table, so that
people can only see them by stepping up to your booth.
Remember, our goal is to sell the bestsellers first.

These niche products work in tandem with your bestsellers
and should only be used as a profit maximizer or to save a
sale. If your bestselling products won't close a deal, then
add these niche products into the mix to reinvigorate
interest.

The last product you need to include for a successful booth
is your freebie, which lives at the middle of your table.
These can be fliers, prints, buttons, or anything a person
can easily pick up for little to no cost. When people look up
from checking out your freebie product, they will see you
front and center greeting them.

That's because all of these products combine to form a
pathway from the front of the table directly to your eye line
behind it. The customer is not only drawn to your products,
but also to you. Setting up your table in this manner forces
more intimate interactions with more potential customers.
The more interactions you have, the more sales you will
make.

Customers have an impossible time making a buying
decision. If you feed them too many choices, they'll
eventually give up and walk away. If you focus on
maximizing sales of a few products, you will find that your
overall sales increase, as do your margins.

If for some reason customers don't want any of the
products on your table, you can always guide them to the
perfect piece tucked away in storage underneath your table.

Those customers trust you more because you took the time to listen, and are thus more likely to buy from you.

SPLITTING TABLES

I will split any table at any convention. I will split an eight-by-six or even a four-foot table to keep costs down. One time I even split a twenty-dollar table. There has never been a con where I wouldn't rather split a table than go it alone. Splitting tables is one of the best ways to maximize con sales while minimizing costs.

I'm an anomaly in that respect. Most creatives have a problem splitting tables. They believe if they don't have a full table, they're somehow less of an exhibitor. Or that they need a full table because they have too much stuff to split one. Or because they don't want somebody taking their sales.

These are all misplaced fears.

Is there a chance you could make more money with a full table? Of course, but there are downsides and pitfalls to every situation. The key is to weigh the benefits with the drawbacks. When you are first starting out, the benefits to splitting tables are numerous. It behooves you to look into table splitting even if you are further along in your career. The benefits extend beyond just saving money.

That's not to say that saving money isn't a primary reason why I split as many tables as possible. Cost was the key reason I started splitting tables in the first place. Especially when you start out, the chances you'll make three hundred dollars back on a table are minimal. You probably don't even have enough inventory to make a three-hundred-dollar investment worthwhile. It's much more likely you'll make about a hundred dollars on a table, give or take. Even if you don't make any money, losing a hundred dollars is more palatable than losing three hundred.

The benefits don't stop at saving money, though.

By splitting a table, you don't need to bring as much stuff to a convention. This is great for newbies, because you probably won't have very much inventory in the beginning, but even if you are experienced, this is a great way to identify your bestsellers and niche products.

It's amazing how innovative you become with limited space. I figured out my bestselling products specifically because I had a space issue. I have been splitting space since my first con, so it was always tricky to make my table shine. That limitation forced me to design my booth to maximize the sales of just a few products. Without that constraint, I never would have discovered how to set up my booth for maximum impact.

Aside from sales, you also have somebody to watch your table if you need to run to the bathroom or just want to walk the floor. When you split a table, you can even practice each other's sales pitch and sell things for each other. There's nothing better than coming back to a table and being handed a wad of money from your booth mate.

Yes, you can bring a helper to a convention instead and achieve the same goal, but then you are investing both your time and their time without defraying any of the cost. If you split a table with somebody, then both of you are invested in the same goal while also saving on the table cost.

 Then, there's the companionship that comes along with splitting tables. Sometimes, cons are slow, crappy, and lonely. It's nice to have somebody behind the table, right next to you, to share in your joys and pain. Yes, there are exhibitors on either side of you, but it's not the same. They are busy doing their own thing.

When you split a table, you guys are a team, and that camaraderie is essential to keeping a positive mindset at conventions. Again, you could bring a helper instead of splitting a table, but you have to weigh the pros and cons of whether that extra cost is worthwhile. Splitting the table instead gets you almost the same result and saves you money.

Splitting a table is also beneficial, because you can work together to refer ideal customers to each other. Not everyone is going to love your work. By splitting a table, you have somebody right next to you who can make a sale if a customer isn't feeling your work. If you split a table with the right person, your audiences will be very different. Instead of stealing sales, you can help find each other's ideal customer.

I personally love tabling with people who have all-ages material, because our Wannabe Press books are for mature readers. Therefore, anybody coming to my table and looking for all-ages books is out of luck, but if I table with an all-ages publisher, we can work in tandem to maximize sales. They send me their mature readers and I send them my all-ages ones. This way, we are both making sales without stepping on each other's toes.

One of the main issues I run into with people who fear table splitting is that they don't want somebody ruining their sales. I have found the opposite to be true. When you split a table, it allows you to work together to make more sales. As a team, you can sell to more customers and make more money. If your work is different enough, then you can complement each other and increase your convention sales. This takes practice and time, but with the right table mate,

you can really maximize sales while minimizing costs—
and that is a beautiful thing.

PACKING A CON KIT

A con kit is an essential part of any exhibitor's convention prep. A con kit is simply a pre-prepared bag of essentials you create before leaving your house. Most items in your kit stay there permanently. I keep my con kit in my car at all times, so I never have to remember it. Every few months I take stock and refill as needed. Otherwise, I don't even think about it.

Every exhibitor has a different style to their kit, but there are certain things common among everybody on the con circuit. Add or subtract anything you want, but if you start with these essentials, you'll have a great base when you reach the convention floor and never freak out because you forgot something.

Food – The most important part to maintaining a positive attitude at a con is an adequate stash of food. The lunch grumpies are a real thing. They hit congoers and exhibitors alike every day around 12:30. Your choices are either to leave your booth and seek out food or bring it with you.

You can buy food on the convention floor, but it's overpriced and terrible for you. It's much better for your wallet—and stomach—to visit a grocery store and pick up some sandwiches, fruit (I prefer grapes. They pack a burst of sugar and liquid without messing up your hands.), nuts, granola bars, and a big jug of water.

The sandwiches and fruit are one of the only parts of your kit that you can't keep in your car at all times. The rest of the food might get a little hot, but at least it will be edible.

Medical supplies – If you go to enough cons, you will get injured. You should always have band aids of varying sizes, Neosporin, and gauze on hand to mend any injuries that happen to you or your table mates. You also want to have some Aspirin and any other prescription meds you might need to get through the day.

I travel with a couple of knee wraps, too. If you have any joint problems, ace bandages or braces are a must.

Medical supplies also include any hygiene products like tampons you might need either now or in the future. Even if you won't need them for your next con, you will need them eventually.

Hand sanitizer – Cons are full of disease. You'll be interacting with tons of people every day. If you don't have hand sanitizer, you will get sick. You will probably get sick anyway.

Grooming products – You'll probably be out late after the con closes or at the very least feel haggard at some point during a long con day. When that happens, it's always nice to splash some water on your face, comb your hair, put on some fresh deodorant, and touch up your makeup before you head back onto the floor. It can make you feel like a new person.

If you can't get to the bathroom, then baby wipes are a convenient way to get a bit of relief while at your table. That momentary refreshment can turn your whole day around.

I don't go back to my room after the convention floor closes. I head straight to the next event, so having a way to get ready for the evening at my table is essential. Toothbrush, toothpaste, or at least mouthwash make me feel like at least I tried a little bit, even if I didn't really.

Ziplock baggies – Make sure all your leakable products are stowed safely in ziplock bags so they don't destroy your entire kit. Bring a couple extras, too, just in case.

Surge protector and extension cord – You won't usually have power, but it's nice to have an extension cord and surge protector just in case you find a magical outlet somewhere.

Battery Pack – Since electricity costs money at cons, your electronics will inevitably die. That is a guarantee. Make sure to have an additional battery pack or flash charger ready so you can keep going without worrying about a dead battery. These need to be charged every night of the con to make sure they aren't dead when you need them. If you want to guarantee power at your table, aim for a 10,000 mAh or higher battery with extra cords.

Cash – It's always good to have a small stash of cash in your con kit in case you don't get a chance to hit up an ATM. I always keep different denominations in my wallet since I go to so many cons. If you aren't a frequent exhibitor, though, it's nice to have it in your kit so you don't forget. For some reason I settled on $140 equally split between tens and fives, but every exhibitor has a different amount they bring to cons.

Scissors – There will be things to open at your table that require scissors. I fear cutting myself when I reach into my bag, so I bring rounded scissors like a child would use. I know that's a crazy fear, especially since rounded scissors can barely cut soft cheese, but I've almost stabbed myself too many times to risk anything sharper.

Tape – Every con has things that need mending, merchandise that needs hanging, and broken things that need fixing. That's why tape is an essential part of any con kit. I recommend bringing multiple kinds: masking, duct, packing, and scotch. They each serve a different function, and you want to be sure to have the right tape for the right job.

Art supplies – There are always a couple artists at every con who forget their brushes and at least one author who runs out of sharpies. You don't have to load your entire studio into your kit, but you should create a packet of essential supplies just in case the worst happens.

Chair cushions and floor pads – Con floors are made of concrete and terrible on your legs. Con chairs are miserable for your back and butt. You will be standing and sitting all day on the worst surfaces imaginable. Chair cushions and floor pads can make that experience much easier to endure.

Card reader – You need a card reader to take credit card payments. While you can manually punch in the card, the reader makes it so much easier for you and the customer. I currently use Square, but I've used PayPal in the past with great success, too.

Tablet for mailing list – Especially at a big convention, you want to have a separate tablet for your mailing list that isn't your phone. Your phone will be taking credit card payments, and it can only do one thing at a time. You want to make sure fans can sign up quickly and without waiting. Additionally, anything you can do to help prevent battery drain on your phone is a good thing.

Needle and thread – If you don't want to look like a hobo when something tears, pack a needle and thread to fix any holes that pop up in either your table or your clothes.

That's right. You have to worry about more than just your table at these conventions; your clothes can tear, too. When they do, it's not a pleasant experience. Having a needle and thread on hand is way better than trying to fix your clothes with tape or leaving it unattended for everybody to see.

This is not an all-encompassing list. Your needs will differ over time and depending on what you sell. The con kit for an exhibitor booth is much different than for an artist table, and people who make pillows have different needs than those who sell books.

This is only a starting point. Add and subtract as necessary. I know it feels like overkill, but it's better to have something and not need it than need something and not have it.

HOW TO MARKET YOURSELF AS AN EXHIBITOR

Once you've honed your products and perfected your pitch, it's time to set up the rest of the table. This is the marketing aspect of exhibiting at a convention. It's not about salesmanship. It's about getting people's attention and driving them to your booth without saying a word. Your salesmanship and marketing work together to create an irresistible experience for your ideal customer.

The first piece of crafting that experience is an eye-catching **table drape**. A table drape goes over your table and covers up all the ugly bits underneath like overflow merchandise and your con kit.

Many cons provide their own drape, but they are uniform across every table in the convention center. You don't want to be uniform. You want to stand out. In order to do that, you need to invest in your own table drape.

The more unique the table drape, the more it attracts your ideal customer. You don't have to spend a fortune on a drape. Fabric stores have an incredible selection to choose from in every color and design under the sun. If you time it right, you can get an awesome deal on prints that stores want to unload.

If you want to get fancy, you can order a custom pattern from Spoonflower for a very reasonable price. I use Spoonflower for all my table drapes. It ensures I get the perfect color and pattern to fit my needs. I'm willing to spend a little more to make sure I have a custom drape nobody else can mimic.

The next thing your table needs is a **banner**. Banners get very expensive on the high end, but they don't have to be pricey. You can order a cheap banner online for as little as twenty dollars, and hang it from PVC pipes you find at Home Depot using zip ties.

I'm all about convenience, though, which is why I bought a retractable banner. They take very little time to set up and immediately make you look like a pro. They are also very compact. Since I split my tables every chance I get and usually don't have much space, retractable stands are the best option for me.

Your booth also needs a **display** for your products. This can be as simple as a wire stand or as complicated as a homemade box. The display needs to fit with your overall aesthetic, raise your products off the ground, and entice people to interact with what you are offering them.

The final piece of marketing you need for your table is a collection of **freebies**. A freebie is something you hand out as people pass by your table. Everybody is looking for a freebie, and your customers are no different. You need two different types of freebies to create the most successful table experience.

The first freebie is one you hand out to everybody who passes by your table. It should have the same messaging as the rest of your booth. The goal of this freebie is to connect your flier with the customer's experience at your table. For our promotional flier, we have the Wannabe Press mascot, along with every book the customer saw at our table. The background of the flier is the same green color as our table drape and banner.

The second freebie is one you use to sign people up for your mailing list. This is the freebie offer we talked about earlier. It isn't actually a freebie, per se. It's a product you've priced below five dollars and are willing to give away for free when somebody signs up for your mailing list.

This second freebie doesn't have to match your coloring, but it should complement your branding. We use our Wannabe mascot in all our mailing list freebies. As long as somebody stays on our mailing list, they can always get our mailing list freebies without paying a dime. It's a way to reward our fans while building brand loyalty. MailChimp uses a similar tactic with their own monkey mascot.

Those are the mandatory marketing pieces you need for your booth. If you want to supercharge your marketing, though, holding special events at your table are your best friend. These can be live draws, raffles, or even an exclusive signing. These events signal to your ideal customer that your booth is a place to congregate. They create a reason for people to come to your booth and, more importantly, a reason for them to return throughout the weekend.

The final piece of your con marketing is social media integration. If you are using Buffer, Hootsuite, or similar programs, start scheduling posts a week before the con. Post at least once every day for the week leading up to the convention. Once the con starts, increase your social media posts to three times a day so people know where you are and what you're doing.

While you're there, take pictures of cosplayers, people who buy your products, and other cool stuff you see around the convention center. Make sure to include your booth number in every post. Check for any trending hashtags related to the show—people search those to find cool stuff. If they think your booth is a happening place, they'll be more likely to check out your table or at least follow you for future events.

If you have a mailing list, send out a newsletter update with the exact location of where you will be on the convention floor. Make sure to include a map so your fans have no problem finding your booth location. While you're at it, make that map the cover image on all your social media accounts so people can easily reference it.

I want to end this section by talking about whether or not you should put prices on your merchandise. It's one of the main places where I differ from almost every other creator on the con circuit. Most people tell you to price everything on the table. I wholeheartedly disagree.

Here's why.

The minute somebody sees pricing, they make a snap judgement on whether to stop by your booth based on that price. As an independent creator, your work will be priced higher than almost everybody else at the convention.

That means you are competing with other people on price, even though you can't possibly win that battle. Since you can't compete on price, you shouldn't put prices on your product. Instead, you should compete with them on value and quality.

People don't know the value of your product right away, so you need to engage them in conversation to entice them. Once they talk to you, handle your product, and understand the quality of your work, you can then tell them the price and have a better chance of making the sale.

All of this marketing is useless if you don't have an awesome product and haven't honed your pitch. When combined with a perfect sales pitch and amazing content, though, these marketing elements can cement you, in the mind of your customers, as a brand worthy of attention.

HOW TO MARKET YOURSELF AS AN ATTENDEE

Creators don't start going to cons as exhibitors right off the bat. Everyone I've ever met started going as an attendee. It only makes sense. Attending cons is a great way to meet people and gather market research without investing money on an expensive table.

However, most creators don't understand "con etiquette" when they get started. There are rules you need to follow to make the most of a con. If you can nail these, you'll be well on your way to making incredible connections that can last a lifetime. If you don't, you will become nothing but a forgettable footnote.

Buy something from exhibitors when you ask their advice.

Some creators make 50 percent or more of their income from attending shows. They aren't there to have fun. They are there to work. If you are sitting by their table for a half hour, people are less likely to stop by their booth. Therefore, they are losing money.

Every minute you take of their time costs money. Which is fine. We all expect questions. Most of us relish them, but time is money. If you like the creator, buy something from their table to show them you value their time and advice.

I always tell people that twenty dollars buys five minutes of my undivided attention. When I was attending cons, I made sure to bring two hundred dollars to buy time from people I respected. I wanted to make a good impression with them, and buying from their work showed I valued their advice.

This also solves a problem for you. If you get advice from a creator, you want to know if that advice is quality, right? You'll only know that by testing out their products. If the product is great, then you know the advice is solid. If it's crappy, though, you should probably discount it and move on to another creator.

Ask intelligent questions about their work.

Creators bend over backwards for fans. If you've read somebody's work, let them know before you start asking questions. If you do that, you will get much more out of your interactions than if you just start pelting them with questions.

Don't say something generic, either. Your questions need to be specific. Everybody says, "I like your work." If you can say, "I really liked when you did X. What was the reason behind that?" it's going to make you stand out from the crowd.

If you give a creator something to review, understand that they won't look at it until after the con.

I love getting handouts and books from people. I read everything that people give me. It's impossible to read anything until I get home and decompress for a couple days. I just don't have the bandwidth to critique anything until I've had a chance to recharge.

Giving notes is a part of my brain that just doesn't function at shows. If I tell you to email me later, though, I mean it. I'm not blowing you off. Please respect that. If you get indignant, I'm just going to toss what you gave me in the trash. I don't have time for that kind of attitude.

If somebody tells you to email them, do it.

I tell every creator I meet to email me their questions and I will gladly answer them. Do you know how often people take me up on that offer?

Never.

I've received a total of ten emails this year out of thousands of people I've told to email me. If you are a creator and somebody tells you to get in touch with them…do it!

Tuck their card away in your wallet, wait a couple of weeks, and then email your questions. You'll be shocked at the response you receive because nobody else is doing it.

I can only devote a couple minutes to somebody at a show. After a show I can give so much more. Plus, I can really think about the answers to your questions.

If you actually take the initiative and email creators, they will notice. Maybe not all of them, but enough of them to make a difference in your career.

If you pitch somebody a project, keep it brief and informative.

Many creators attend shows to find artists and writers to work on their projects. Cons are a great way to put a face to an email and quickly move a project into production.

However, you must be prepared when meeting with somebody. Exhibitors are very busy and extremely tired.

They've been working the con floor for hours. They don't have the energy for long, rambling soliloquies.

If you meet somebody interested in working with you, be succinct. Make sure to have a budget in mind, a quick pitch of your project, and a timeline in place for the start of production.

Additionally, prepare a one-page document containing all the pertinent information so they can review it after the convention.

Then, decide with them when to follow up to talk about your project. Your entire pitch should take less than two minutes.

Just because somebody isn't jumping for joy at your pitch doesn't mean they aren't interested. It might just mean they are braindead from hours on the con floor.

Scope out the hip after-hour spots.

Every big convention has a bar where exhibitors go after the floor closes. If you can find that spot, you can talk to artists and authors when their guard is down. Just remember to be considerate. This isn't a time for pitching. It's a time for mingling. Standard cocktail party rules apply.

Follow creators on social media before the con begins and engage with them.

The more points of contact you have with somebody before an event, the most likely they are to remember you at the convention. So, start before the convention even begins. Favorite things they say on social media. Tweet at them. Be engaged. Just like above, this isn't about pitching. It's about engaging.

The more cons you attend, the more seriously exhibitors will take you.

There is a cumulative effect that builds the more often people see you at conventions. If you go to enough shows, creators will take you more seriously, especially if you've completed more and more quality projects with each interaction.

This is because the brain forms connections between the number of times it sees a person and its perceived friendship level with them. You can actually become friends with somebody just by being present enough times and having positive interactions with them on each occasion, just like we talked about before.

Even if you don't have success at your first show, traction builds exponentially over time as people interact with you more and more. If you show up at conventions long enough, you will inevitably move from attendee to colleague to friend in the eyes of many people who can help catapult your career forward.

If you follow these tips, you will be much more successful in meeting people at cons and making positive connections with them. The more times you attend shows and talk with creators, the stronger those connections will become and the further you will get in your career.

SPEAK TO SELL

One of the most underutilized secrets to succeeding at live events is that speaking on panels and giving workshops helps you sell more, not less. Even though you are away from your booth for an hour, you make up for the loss of potential sales with the quality of leads gained from your speaking engagements.

This logic is rooted deep in the principles of your sales funnel.

The goal of your sales funnel is to get people to know, like, and trust you, so that they are more likely to buy from you. At your table, you can only talk with somebody for a couple of minutes. In a panel room, though, you have the undivided attention of your audience for an hour. This allows for a much deeper engagement with the people in your panel than you could ever get at your table.

In fact, speaking on panels gives you the deepest engagement possible with attendees, while helping you stand out from other exhibitors. Panels help attendees develop a personal connection with your brand, fueling their desire to buy your product.

Additionally, panels allow you to leverage the convention's authority and transfer it to yourself. You have been chosen to represent the convention by its organizers. Since attendees respect the authority of the convention, that authority rubs off on you when you are on a panel.

On top of using the authority of the convention, panel attendees commit to your brand by agreeing to sit in on your panel instead of walking the convention floor or attending another event.

As you sit on the panel and deliver valuable advice to the audience, you build up your likability with them, and because you have given them something without asking for anything in return, attendees develop reciprocity with your brand.

The size of the audience builds up your social proof as an expert who knows what they are doing. By simply sitting on panels, you've hit five of the six essential buying triggers without lifting a finger.

So…how do we get onto panels?

I used to think it was an impossible task. There were so many people better qualified than me to speak about creating and selling books; however, I quickly learned that most people don't like presenting on panels. They either think it's a waste of their time or have a crippling fear of public speaking.

I couldn't believe it, but I wasn't about to argue.

If you want to start booking yourself onto panels, I've developed several strategies to maximize this very lucrative part of live events.

The best way to get on a panel is by moderating one. To do that, you need to contact the event organizers and fill out a panel request form. You are responsible for finding the panelists beforehand and picking the topic. Organizers have tons of time slots to fill in their programming schedule, so if you put together a great list of panelists and an interesting topic their audience will enjoy, there is a great chance they will book your panel.

Even if you don't book a panel beforehand, it's always a good idea to find the panel organizer when you get to the show and ask if they have any openings you can fill. Often, people have to cancel at the last minute and you play hero by helping them in their hour of need.

The easiest way to start booking panels is to simply walk into the room a couple minutes before a panel starts and ask the moderator if they have room for another panelist. You would be surprised how often this works if you carry yourself with confidence and have a smile on your face. Even if it doesn't work the first time, it will work eventually if you ask enough people.

If you aren't comfortable walking right up to the moderator in the panel room, check out the panel schedule when you first get to the convention, figure out which panels you qualify for, and then find the moderator's booth.

It takes a little investigation, but you can often find their booths if you cross- reference their names on social media. Many exhibitors post their booth numbers on Twitter or Facebook before the con starts. If you can't find it on their social media feed, check out the con's website. Most cons have a webpage dedicated to their floor plan and exhibitor list.

Once you know the moderator's booth number, make it a point to find them before their panel and make a connection with them so they will consider booking you for future events.

The most reliable way to book speaking engagements is to start small. Small shows are always desperate for programming help. They never have enough staff to devote to booking panels. Therefore, if you ask small shows to host a panel, they are often more than happy for you to take that responsibility off their shoulders.

I began speaking at a small local show called Long Beach Comic Con many years ago. My role in their programming grew along with the size of the show. I started by hosting one panel, and now I organize four to six panels for them a year. Building on that experience, I was then able to contact other shows and use Long Beach as a reference point. Each time I spoke at a new convention, it gave me access to bigger and bigger shows, including San Diego Comic-Con.

Speaking engagements are often the last piece to come together in a successful con strategy. You must be known by exhibitors and con organizers alike before you can book panels consistently, but that doesn't mean you shouldn't start immediately. Just remember, speaking isn't only about fun. It's also about moving people down your funnel in a calculated and effective way. If you book speaking engagements with that mentality, it can be a very lucrative way to build your audience.

BIG CONS VS. SMALL CONS

I have friends who spend over $5,000 attending one convention a year. Of course, that convention is San Diego Comic-Con and they get a huge booth, but they blow their entire marketing wad on one show. That means for the rest of the year, they have no budget to do anything else except social media outreach, which has a much lower conversion rate.

Meanwhile, I have roughly the same show budget, but I am able to attend almost fifty shows a year. This is because I'm always looking for ways to lower my table cost so I can exhibit at more shows.

For instance, I spend $500 on a small press table at Comic-Con instead of $5000 on a booth, and then I split that table in half with the creators I publish through Wannabe Press. That means I'm spending $250 on a table at the same convention where other exhibitors are spending five grand.

That gives me $4750 more a year to attend additional shows, from big shows like WonderCon, all the way down to local library shows down the street. While huge conventions are the anchor points of a successful show strategy, small conventions are the backbone of exponential brand growth.

The truth is that you need to consistently table at shows if you want to stay current in the minds of your audience. There just aren't enough big shows to sustain a consistent brand presence. Even in Los Angeles, there are only three or four anchor shows a year. The rest of my con strategy involves filling in those gaps with local shows.

Smaller conventions don't bring the cash windfall of a show like San Diego Comic-Con, but they also don't cost nearly as much to attend. Instead of paying $5,000 for an exhibitor booth at an enormous show, most small shows cost less than $50 to attend. Many cons will even offer you a free table.

This means that with the same $5,000 budget, I can attend upwards of fifty shows or more a year instead of just a single one. It's true a huge exhibitor booth will get more exposure than a small press table at any given show, but they don't get fifty times the exposure. Even if they do, that exposure is limited to a single week, whereas my exposure is spread out over an entire year.

Of course, this doesn't mean you should only attend small cons, either. Your con schedule should be made up of a combination of small and large conventions, as they each serve different purposes.

Large shows give your brand legitimacy in the eyes of your ideal customers. By going to shows that people recognize—like Emerald City Comic Con, Phoenix, New York Comic Con, WonderCon, and San Diego Comic-Con—you immediately build your authority and social proof with your ideal customer even if you never meet them in person.

The brand recognition alone is worth the price of admission; however, don't feel the need to buy an enormous booth at a big convention to legitimize yourself. Brand recognition works equally well whether you buy a huge booth or the smallest table possible. In the eyes of your online audience, there is no difference.

Exhibiting at a huge convention can supercharge your mailing list growth, too. While I get around twenty new mailing list subscribers at a small convention, I add over two hundred at a larger one.

Additionally, larger cons give you the best chance to network with large publishers, well-known creators, agents, managers, producers, and press outlets. While some of these movers and shakers attend smaller conventions, bigger cons bring them out of the woodwork.

The downside to big cons is that they are a meat market. You can't talk to any one person for more than a couple of minutes. At big cons, you make your money by the sheer volume of people walking past your table. Smaller cons, on the other hand, allow you to have more meaningful conversations with attendees.

A small con allows you to talk with a single person for a long time. You can talk with attendees in depth about your product and build a real connection with them. At these smaller cons, you make your money by the quality of your engagement. I use small cons to build incredible value and empathy with attendees. I often meet customers at a larger convention, but they don't buy until they find me at a smaller one.

This is the key value of varying up your convention strategy with both large and small cons. Because you can exhibit at more conventions, you build up more brand awareness and likability than if you only exhibit at large cons.

The main reason Wannabe Press is so successful at conventions is because people see us over and over again. I can't tell you how many people we talk to at conventions who mention originally meeting us at a different con from months earlier. Eventually, people who meet us over and over again become customers simply because we've treated them with respect; we've moved to the top of their buy list by being consistently present in their mind.

A customer needs to be touched seven to fifteen times by a company in order to become a client. A touch point could be your newsletter, a post on social media, or an advertisement; however, the most powerful touch point is always in-person communication. There is no substitute for looking somebody in the eyes and shaking their hand to build an instant connection with them.

Unless you travel, which is extremely expensive, there aren't enough big shows in any given area to consistently reach out to your potential audience in person. Therefore, to maintain those in-person relationships, you must attend smaller shows, as well.

To find smaller shows, ask at your local comic book shops and build a network of local creators. They are the best sources to find local shows. If you create a good group of people in the know, you will be surprised how many small shows pop up in your area. If you work together, you can dominate the local con market. If you try to go it alone, you will most likely struggle.

PART 5

LAUNCHING A SUCCESSFUL PRODUCT

In order to have a successful product launch, it's important to internalize the belief that your creative work is, in essence, a product, just like any other product on the market. It's a product unique to your creative mind, but a product nonetheless.

Coming to terms with this fact was one of the hardest struggles of my creative life. My work is very personal to me; my finished creations represent a piece of my soul and a part of my heart. I pour everything into my work, and pushing it out into the world was once too difficult for my ego to bear.

I know that's hard to believe, but my ego is as fragile as any other artist's. It's precious and tiny and prone to break with even the lightest touch. The only difference between me and most other artists is that I've been able to separate the creation of my work from the selling of it.

Make no mistake, though, I fear the same rejection. I face the same doubt. It's a natural part of the creative process. At the end of the day, you are giving a piece of your soul to somebody and asking them to love and care for it.

I am very protective of the creative process. I love it, nurture it, and cherish it. Only after I've finished something completely do I allow my business mind to take over. Once the finished product is in my hands, I cease to be its creator and my brain starts building toward a successful product launch.

This last section of this book is about the final tenet needed to build a successful creative business—how to successfully launch your products into the world. A successful launch validates the salability of your product on the open market, allows you to build traction with your audience, and creates buzz so you can sell your product for years and years to come.

You likely have experience with at least one platform that has successfully launched thousands of products onto the market. That platform is Kickstarter.

I've successfully used Kickstarter multiple times to launch products, and I am a diehard Kickstarter fanatic; however, Kickstarter is by no means the only way to launch. Products launch in all sorts of ways, from Amazon to Shopify, and even on custom-made websites.

You do not have to use Kickstarter in order to have success launching a product. However, I have heavily skewed this chapter with examples from Kickstarter.

I've structured this chapter so that you can use its principle to launch a product on whatever platform works for you. This is the shortest chapter of the book, but not because it's not as important as the others. If anything, it's the most important thing we've discussed so far. This chapter is only short because most of the principles needed to successfully launch a product have been discussed thoroughly in previous chapters.

MAKE DEPOSITS INTO THE GOODWILL BANK

You are going to ask for a lot from your audience when launching a product. They will be bombarded by it on every social media channel imaginable; you will be disseminating information dozens of times a day on multiple outlets. God help the people who follow you on multiple channels. They're the real heroes.

With so many updates about your product, it's easy for people to become annoyed with you and tired of your product. They will want to unsubscribe from your newsletter and unfollow you on social media. By the time your launch is over, they won't want to hear from you ever again.

The only way to combat this is to have a great relationship with your audience before you launch your product, because you will torch it once your launch begins.

That's why you need to be making deposits into the goodwill bank far in advance of any product launch. This is the crux of the value first mentality. This is the business reason for why we have to provide information to our audience and grow their trust before we ask anything in return.

Because we will ask for something in return when we launch a product, and we will ask a lot. We will ask so much that any rational person will tune us out. But emotions aren't rational. People allow those they like and trust to get away with irrational things, like pounding them with reasons to buy their product.

That's why we need to build up massive goodwill before we even consider launching our product.

Think about your goodwill like it's a bank. We'll call it The First Bank of Goodwill. This bank works like any other bank, except that it runs on your goodwill instead of money.

When you do something nice for somebody, you make a deposit into this bank. Whether it's writing a blog post, speaking on a panel, providing advice over coffee, or even just retweeting an interesting article, everything you do for your audience is a deposit in the goodwill bank.

By contrast, everything you ask of your audience is a withdrawal from the goodwill bank. Every time you ask somebody to buy your product, every time you pitch them something, and every single time you ask them to share your posts, you are withdrawing from your goodwill account.

If you have been depositing into the goodwill bank over and over again, you can make these withdrawals without overdrafting your account; however, if you haven't been making these deposits, then you can't afford to make an ask of your audience. Imagine trying to buy a $50,000 boat in cash when your checking account only has $3.27 in it. You just can't do that.

The same is true with your goodwill.

If you keep withdrawing from the goodwill bank without making deposits, there will be nothing left in your account when you need it. Without enough goodwill, your product launch won't be successful, because your audience has no reason to support you. If you keep making those deposits, then you will always have enough goodwill in your account to sustain your withdrawals.

This is where most people screw up when it comes to launching a product. They haven't spent enough time making deposits into the goodwill bank to sustain their withdrawals, so their ask comes across as begging. It's perceived as brash and creates an uncomfortable situation. Instead of people gladly buying the product, they either bristle at the thought of buying or only buy out of pity. This type of customer doesn't stick around for the long haul.

This is why making deposits into the goodwill bank is such an important concept. If you do it correctly, you'll always have a massive amount of goodwill available when it's time to launch your product. With that goodwill built up, your audience will gladly buy from you instead of recoiling from your ask.

Just note, making deposits into the goodwill bank is a perpetual task you must perform throughout your career. You can't just use it on your first launch and coast on the interest forever. Your goodwill account is like a checking account—it doesn't build interest.

Luckily, goodwill is easy to deposit if you are a good person who wants to serve your audience. If you come from a place of service and value, then almost everything you do will make a deposit into the goodwill bank.

SETTING UP YOUR SALES PAGE

You can't have a successful launch without a captivating sales page where customers can buy your work. The function of a sales page is to build up a customer's desire to purchase your product by showing them why they need it in their lives.

The most effective sales pages are built after you've spoken with potential customers about your product in the months leading up to your launch. By pitching the product to your ideal customers, you find out their pain points, their wants, their needs, and their objections. You learn the triggers that convert people into buying customers and what wording prevents them from purchasing your product. All of this research becomes essential data when constructing an effective sales page.

An effective sales page is broken down into four parts. I'm going to use Kickstarter to describe these parts and how they relate to each other. If you haven't seen a Kickstarter page, head on over to their site and click through some of the most funded products before continuing on with this lesson.

(Don't worry. The principles I describe here can be used whether you are launching a Kickstarter or creating your own sales page from scratch. Since the Kickstarter platform is, at its core, nothing but a high-converting sales page, it's a great place to build the foundational knowledge of what makes a page successful.)

The first part of any good sales page is an **enthralling video**. A video is the best way to build empathy and trust with your potential customer. It allows them to see and hear you so they can build an instant connection to you as if they'd met you in person.

The video should be the first thing people see when they come to your page, just like it's the first thing you see when you land on a Kickstarter page, where the video is front and center. You can view it without scrolling at all. I call that "above the fold" placement. It's critical that the video, headline, and main description of your product all have above the fold placement.

The instinct of creatives is to shy away from the camera, but to sell your product, you need people to feel a connection with you. While loving your product is essential, making a connection to you is just as important. So, unfortunately, you must be on camera for at least part of your video. Suck it up and get over it. Our goal here isn't to make you comfortable, it's to sell product. You need to be on camera.

Your sales video is a commercial for your product. It needs to be big, bold, and full of motion—it also needs to be short. There is a reason television commercials top out at sixty seconds. People don't have the attention span for much more than that.

You don't have to keep it under sixty seconds, but your video should be well under three minutes. That means it will only show the highlights of your product, its biggest features, and greatest benefits. I use a very simple structure when it comes to creating my sales videos.

1. **Introduction** – The first part of the video is a simple introduction of myself and the product. This takes under ten seconds. It's literally, "Hi. My name is Russell, and I'm the publisher of Wannabe Press.

I'm here to tell you about my awesome, new product."

2. **The Product** – In this section I talk about the product and its biggest features for no more than sixty seconds. I highlight what makes the product unique and why people should buy it. Additionally, I add imagery that pleases the eye and entices people to keep watching. Remember, this is an ad, so it has to engage and entertain the viewer.

3. **The Plea** – After demonstrating the product, the third part of your video contains the exact reasons it needs to exist and why people need to buy it immediately. During my video for the *Spaceship Broken, Needs Repairs* campaign, I explained that I came to Kickstarter specifically because the subject of the book (abuse) was incredibly niche and had no hope of succeeding on the open market without an initial boost from the Kickstarter community. If they didn't support it, then it would never see the open market. Since Kickstarter is a marketplace for weird, new, and original ideas that wouldn't exist on their own, this plea struck a nerve and I was able to fund my fifth successful campaign.

It's a really simple formula that I've used again and again. I've never had a video run over three minutes, and almost all my videos have clocked in under 2:30. The shorter you make the video, the more likely people will be to stay until the end.

The second part of any good sales page is **captivating copy**. Most customers visiting your sales page will start with the video. If they like what they see, then they will quickly jump down to your copy. These are the words that describe your campaign.

On the Kickstarter page, the copy is found directly under the video. The name of the product and main description are above the fold, then you have to scroll down to read any of the product's benefits.

If the sales video is a flashy teaser for your product, then the copy fleshes out all of the reasons somebody should buy your work. It should expound on everything you said in the video, and add even more benefits than what you could fit inside three minutes.

All good copy starts with an eye-catching title and product description. Yes, you need to include the name of your product in the title, but don't be afraid to add a descriptor after the product name to further define it.

For instance, OUYA launched on Kickstarter a few years ago. Unless I told you that it was a video game console, most people would have no idea what OUYA did or why they should buy it. Therefore, when they launched, the title of their product became OUYA: A New Kind of Video Game Console.

The descriptor was a great way to get people invested in their product launch immediately. They instantly defined their market and boosted their clicks with just a couple of words.

The same is true with the logline for your product. If you've been pitching your product for a long time, you'll know exactly how to summarize it for maximum effectiveness. Remember, it's not about the what or how of your product. It's about creating an emotional resonance with your customer so their soul needs to have it.

At the end of the day, copy isn't about you. It's about your customer and why your product is perfect for them. Even when you talk about yourself, it needs to reflect the reasons why you are uniquely qualified to birth your product into the world.

As you move down your page, make sure to break your copy up into distinct paragraphs, each with a main idea, supporting sentences, and a conclusion. Then, compile these paragraphs into easy-to-follow lists that can be read without any guidance.

Customers have been trained to read sales pages like lists, scrolling through until they see something pertinent to them. Because of that, every bullet point needs to be carefully constructed to deal with a specific problem without rambling off topic. Your customers should have all their questions answered by the time they finish reading your copy. If they are still scratching their heads wondering what your product can do for them, you've lost a sale.

The third part of creating a killer sales page is inserting **beautiful images**. Ever hear the phrase "A picture's worth a thousand words?" Well, it's especially true when you are trying to sell something. Images reveal more information about your product than copy ever could.

Additionally, customers associate imagery with professionalism. On Kickstarter pages, images are interspersed with copy to break up thoughts and give customers a relief from word-heavy paragraphs. They also define the key benefits and features of products that would take thousands of words to describe.

The easiest way to make your sales page look more professional is by adding quality imagery. Good sales pages on Kickstarter have five or six images, but the best have ten or more. The more relevant imagery you can have on your sales page, the more positively your customers will view your product.

The final part of creating a killer sales page is **the rewards**. These rewards are what people get for buying your product. On Kickstarter, rewards are placed on the right-hand side of the page so a customer can pledge to a product easily once they have been convinced to buy.

While this is an elegant solution for where to place rewards, most sales pages place their rewards at the bottom of the page instead of along the side, and add a "ready to buy?" link after every few paragraphs that redirects customers to a checkout page.

Wherever you place your rewards, each tier needs to be targeted to a specific type of customer just like we talked about in previous chapters. You should have targeted reward tiers for your tripwire, core product, and profit maximizer buyer personas—remember those from Part Two?

Additionally, always include lower-tier rewards in your higher tiers. It's tempting to make rewards exclusive to a single level, but this prevents people from choosing higher reward levels if they really love something at the lower-tier rewards, and if you don't make your rewards inclusive, then you lose out on that additional revenue. I made this mistake during my first launches, and it prevented several backers from increasing their pledges to higher tiers.

Those are the four parts of a killer sales page. If you can nail those four pieces, you will convince the maximum number of people to buy your product at launch, which in turn will set you up for success in the future.

SETTING UP A MARKETING STRATEGY FOR YOUR LAUNCH

A product launch is like pushing a boulder down a hill. There's no stopping it once it starts, so you want to make sure you are prepared before you nudge it forward.

Most creators derail their campaigns because of the misguided reluctance to bug their fans. Because they choose to be courteous, they end up with a passive marketing campaign, or no campaign at all.

While you will certainly bug some people with a more robust campaign, this belief also prevents customers who really want your product from seeing it enough times to make a buying decision.

Customers need seven to fifteen touch points before they make the decision to buy your product. If you only hit them one or two times over the course of your product launch, you haven't given prospects enough information to push them over the edge.

Think about when Starbucks relaunches their pumpkin spice latte or when McDonald's rolls out the McRib. You see those billboards everywhere and hear those radio spots constantly. That market saturation is how they gather enough touch points to make sure their audience is aware of their product and ready to buy it.

To have a successful launch, you need to plan an aggressive marketing campaign just like Starbucks or McDonalds. One or two updates during your product launch aren't sufficient to gain traction with your audience.

You must plan dozens of touch points daily so customers can interact with your product enough to make a buying decision.

Your marketing strategy needs to be robust, efficient, and it needs to start well before your campaign launches. The exact schedule you employ will vary wildly depending on the size of your audience and your choice of social media channels; however, the necessary elements are always the same.

If you set up these elements well in advance, you can get out in front of the marketing boulder, instead of having it crush you underneath its unstoppable momentum.

Create a sales page with email list opt-in and autoresponder sequence. A couple of months before your campaign begins, set up your sales page with a different opt-in email list than the main list on your website and a new targeted auto-responder sequence that specifically tells people about your new product.

This isn't the same as your main email list. This one is specific to your product. Your first set of emails to this list should introduce customers to your product, its benefits, and why they should get excited about it. Make sure to send regular emails to this list and give them updates on the progress of your product.

Every time you send a newsletter to your main list, make sure to reference your new product sales page so people on your main list can easily migrate to your product's new email list.

The goal of this targeted list is to prime your customers to buy this single, specific product, so hyper-focus your discussions to just the areas of interest for that ideal customer. If you are creating a boat calendar, for instance, then focus your discussion on different kinds of boats that will appear in the calendar.

Start a Facebook group for your product. Months before your campaign launches, set up a Facebook group dedicated to your product. This is where you can show the behind-the-scenes stuff that audiences love.

Design different imagery for every day of the campaign. Your audience is willing to be touched by you, but only if you provide new reasons to touch them. You can't feed them the same imagery and information every day. When planning your launch, make sure to create at least one or two different images for every day of the campaign. This will keep your information fresh throughout your launch and give you new touch points with your audience.

Write new posts for every day of the campaign. You can't plan everything you will say during your campaign updates because launches change constantly; however, you should have the general gist of your daily updates planned in advance. These posts are aimed at people who haven't bought yet, so they should build on each other every day.

For instance, if you sell weight loss pills, you could talk about how tough it is to eat properly on day one, the stress of dieting on day two, and the advantages to diet pills on day three. These three updates build on each other and prime your audience to buy without ever pushing a sale on somebody.

You will always talk about your product at the bottom of your post and provide a link to your sales page, but you need to prime the audience with information before asking for their money.

Hunt down guest posts and podcast appearances. It takes months and thousands of emails to book guest posts and podcast appearances. You might need to send out a hundred emails or more to get a single "yes" from a news outlet.

That's why it's so important to start contacting the press early, give them beta access to your product, and make sure your pitch is on point so they have an easy time saying yes.

Get the most out of these appearances by coordinating with your press contact so they can post your article at a time that will maximize its exposure.

This isn't necessarily at the beginning of your campaign, either. Most creators get the maximum benefit of press during the lull in the middle of their campaign, once their campaign has gained momentum from their existing audience and needs a boost from new customers.

Set up an affiliate program. I highly recommend setting up an affiliate commission program for your launch. An affiliate program allows people to create a unique website link they can share on social media, with their email list, or even through advertising. Every time a customer uses that link to buy your product, the affiliate gets paid. This incentivizes your affiliates to share their unique code often, because every share means money in the bank. The promise of getting paid is a great motivator to get people enthused about spreading the word about your product.

If you use Amazon, your affiliates can use the Amazon affiliate program. If you are using Kickstarter, then use Kickbooster. Indiegogo has a built in affiliate program. If you are launching on Wordpress, you can use WP Affiliate among others.

Most artists bristle at creating affiliate programs, but they are a great way to incentivize people to work with you—especially if those people had no personal connection to you beforehand. Press outlets and people with an existing fan base are much more likely to push your product if they can make a little money with every sale they drive. Cash is a great incentive.

Schedule your posts before your campaign begins. You can't schedule every post in advance, but you need a good base of posts and emails in your pipeline before you ever hit the launch button.

I always schedule at least three posts per day per social channel throughout my campaign, and at least one email every week. That means I have a base of content even if I go into a coma for a month, and I can add more throughout the campaign as time allows.

That's the base of information I set up before I launch a product. I also recommend having posts ready when the following benchmarks are triggered in your campaign.

When somebody backs your campaign – This is an easy touch point to create with your audience. People like to be part of the winning team. If they see other people backing your project, it will build up your social proof and make them want to buy your product, as well.

When you reach sales milestones – You will have sales goals within your campaign. Once you hit those goals, celebrate them. Remember, people want to be part of the winning team. When you celebrate your successes, people will want to buy your product and join in on the fun.

When you unlock new rewards – Certain sales milestones should unlock new benefits for people who buy your product. Customers love free stuff. Every bit of free stuff adds value to your campaign and makes people want to back you more. Additionally, the people who already bought your product will see the extra value and push your product more so they can get additional free stuff.

When rewards are going away – Conversely from above, as your campaign moves forward, certain early bird rewards will go away. That scarcity makes people want to back sooner than they might otherwise so they don't lose out on free stuff.

When the campaign begins – It's incredible how many people don't blast their audience when their campaign starts. You must send out emails, updates, and private messages when your campaign begins so people know to back early. Those first few days are critical to your success.

When your campaign is about to end – When your campaign is wrapping up, send out updates like a madman. I send them out the day before, twelve hours before, two hours before, and thirty minutes before the end of any campaign. I want to make sure people know my campaign is about to be over and that they will never be able to get as good a deal on my product, or get any of my other exclusive rewards, ever again.

If you can set up all of these marketing elements early, you will have a rock solid foundation when you hit the launch button. You don't want to get caught without any strategy when your campaign begins, because then you will be scrambling to catch up, which never works. You need to get out in front of your marketing if you want any chance of success.

SURVIVING THE LULL

No matter if you run a Kickstarter, set up a preorder campaign on Amazon, or launch your own website, there will be a lull in the middle of your launch where you don't make very much money. In fact, 75 percent of your funds will come in the first and last few days of your campaign.

There are huge spikes at the beginning and end of your campaign. The beginning spike is because your product is new and exciting. You have built up interest among your ardent fans until they are frothing at the mouth to buy your product.

The end spike happens because people don't want to miss out on buying your product. Their desire to buy has finally overcome their inherent laziness. The scarcity buying trigger comes into play on its own at this point, and people's FOMO (fear of missing out) causes them to back in higher numbers than ever before as your campaign comes to a close.

In the middle of your campaign, however, there is nothing pushing your customers to buy. Your audience knows there is more time to back your campaign and thus they decide to sit on their hands. Your goal, then, is to survive the lull between the beginning and end of your campaign by increasing the number of backers who buy your product in those intervening weeks.

There are many ways to survive the lull, but the most important is to increase the sales at the beginning of your campaign. The more money you make during the initial days of your campaign, the higher your sales will be during the lull. If you can double your sales during the initial spike of your campaign, you can double the sales during the lull, as well.

One of the most effective ways to increase sales at the beginning of your campaign is to offer early bird perks for customers who buy your product in the first three days of your launch.

These perks can be anything from exclusive prints, to a personal call with you, to a wallpaper that customers can only get by committing to your product early in the launch cycle. It's important to make these perks feel special, personal, and unique so that buyers want them. Otherwise, their inherent laziness will take over and they won't make a move until later in your campaign, if at all.

I recommend having three early bird perks on the first day, and removing one each day of your campaign until there are none left. This gives people who buy on day two and three a reason to pledge early, while still rewarding those who backed even earlier with more exclusive stuff. If you drop all your rewards after day one, then people who didn't back on day one have no reason to pledge early. If you give a customer a reason to postpone buying your product, they will take it.

Once you have created a massive spike at the beginning of your campaign, it's time to work on other ways to survive the lull. All of these strategies have one thing in common. They give your audience a reason to check in with you throughout the campaign while increasing their desire for your product to succeed.

Create daily giveaways for your existing backers.

Giving people something for free is a great way to increase their desire to buy your product. I've already talked about how successfully this strategy can be deployed through offering early bird perks to people who buy in the first days of your campaign, but you can sustain that desire and enthusiasm throughout your campaign by offering daily giveaways to your backers.

Every additional day a customer is part of your campaign, they have another chance to win free stuff. This gives people sitting on the fence a reason to back immediately instead of waiting until the end, because their early support means they have more chances to win.

These giveaways don't have to be big spends on your part, but they should be hyper-targeted to your ideal customer so they enthusiastically buy your product early.

You don't have to keep these giveaways confined to just your product, either. If you are creating a sci-fi book, you can buy *Star Wars* Pez dispensers to give away, or *Firefly* bobbleheads. Just remember, if you add things like that to packages, then they no longer qualify for media mail shipping.

Perform weekly challenges for the delight of your audience.

Another of my favorite strategies is performing weekly challenges for my backers. I humiliate myself during campaigns for the benefit of my audience. I have eaten whole onions, recorded humiliating dance moves, created custom ringtones—and more—all for the pleasure of my backers.

The only people who can see these challenges are the customers who have pledged to my campaign. This helps me entice people to get off their butts during the lull so they can see me humiliate myself more times. It's a very effective way to lure your existing audience to join in on the fun, but even new customers like seeing me make an idiot of myself.

Be present for your audience throughout the campaign.

Being present for your audience is a great way to boost enthusiasm for your product among potential customers and give your campaign a human face. This can mean live Q and A's through Facebook Live or Google Hangouts. It could mean AMAs through Reddit, or anywhere you are available for your audience either online or in person.

During my last campaign, I recorded a new Kickstarter tip every day and followed that up with a Facebook Live session every evening to answer questions.

Work with other people who've launched similar products.

If you've built a solid network of creators before you launch a product, you will have friends further along in their career than you who have already launched similar products to people in your ideal audience.

Reach out to them and ask if they will share your product with their audience. Usually, they will offer to share your post on their social media channels. This is nice, but your goal should be to get in front of their email list.

This is where affiliate links can be very effective. Most people don't want to share their email list with anybody, but if you can entice them with money, they are more likely to say yes because you have given them a monetary stake in your success.

Plan your guest blogging strategically to maximize effectiveness.

We've talked about this before, but it's worth mentioning again. When you work with the press, it's important to schedule posts for maximum effectiveness. It does little good to release multiple articles on the same day.

Articles are most effective when they trickle out over the course of your campaign, and you are responsible for making sure they are scheduled properly.

You can't expect the press to magically know when to launch your article for maximum effectiveness. It's your job to take the reins and ensure articles release when they will most effectively influence your ideal audience to make a buying decision.

To survive the lull in the middle of your campaign, you need the enthusiasm of your audience, your network, and your press contacts. You can't do it alone. You have to engage your customer's buying triggers, be present for them when they are ready to buy, and develop a plan to make it enticing for people to back your product in those murky areas between the initial launch and the last days of your campaign.

BUDGETING

It's not a sexy topic, but budgeting for your product launch is one of the most important things you can do to make sure your launch stays on track. A crappy budget will kill your profitability and could even lead to bankruptcy.

I've seen many successfully funded products go awry because they didn't budget properly. When that happens, either the creator has to reach into their own pocket to fulfill their obligations or abandon their project altogether, effectively torching their goodwill for years to come.

Luckily, with a little preparation, a good budget is easy to assemble. All it takes is some elbow grease, diligence, and an ability to google things. Any good budget has seven fundamental sections to it.

Product creation – The product creation section of your budget involves the costs to design your product from scratch into a viable commodity, including purchasing materials, hiring of designers, outsourcing of art, and prototyping a single completed version of your product.

This is not the mass market production of your product. This is everything that goes into getting your product mass market ready, from the packaging to the designing, and the research to the prototyping, so that you can mass produce it in the next section.

Product creation also includes the production of any and all materials associated with your campaign, including stretch goals for any crowdfunding campaigns.

Production – Once your prototype is complete, the second section of your budget deals with the mass market production of your product.

This includes all the setup fees, mass market assembly, and initial shipping of your product to your warehouse. This step takes your product from prototype to a mass market version ready for distribution.

It's important to have at least three different quotes when sourcing production facilities. You need a quote for a minimum run of your product, a second quote for your anticipated run, and a third for your wildly ambitious production run.

You also want to plan for any special additions you might want to add to your product if you hit certain benchmarks. For books, this might include adding spot UV or upgrading to hardcover. For art prints, you might throw in a glass printed version. These additions might also include other stretch goals, too, like T-shirts and hats.

If you are creating additional pieces of apparel like T-shirts or hats along with your core product, make sure they are accounted for in your production budget. Otherwise, you will have a massive budget overage when it comes to producing those pieces and risk bankruptcy.

Additionally, source multiple quotes from facilities that have handled your specific type of product before. Don't cheap out on somebody who says they have experience. Make them prove it. Too many budgets have gone off the rails because creators hired inexperienced production houses simply because they were cheap, and ended up paying thousands of extra dollars to fix errors, effectively bankrupting their launch.

Distribution – Once you have the production costs handled, the third section of your budget is the distribution of your product. This starts with warehousing your product and extends to shipping out your product domestically and across the world.

Warehousing can range from storing your product in your garage, to renting out a storage unit, to working with a fulfillment facility, to buying warehouse space. Amazon has also become a viable option for many creators.

Your needs will depend on how much you expect to produce. Just like with your production run, have contingencies for your minimum, anticipated, and overly ambitious production runs.

When it comes to shipping, take material costs into account along with shipping fees. Bubble mailers are much cheaper than boxes, and buying tape in bulk is much cheaper per unit than buying one roll at a time. Additionally, toner ink and paper cost money—as do setup fees on sites like Backerkit and at distribution facilities like Shipstation.

Once you have warehousing and materials locked down, it's time to tackle shipping costs. You have several options when it comes to mailing a package. For anything involving media, like DVDs, CDs, or books, you can send your shipment media mail in the United States. This is the absolute cheapest way to send anything anywhere, but it is very restrictive to pieces of media and nothing else. Unlike other types of mail, you consent to having the post office open your mail and inspect it so they can ensure you are using the service correctly.

If you can't use media mail, there are several other mail options I won't go into here, except to say that domestic and international shipping rates increase all the time.

Expect rates to change every three to six months. Plan a 10–20 percent buffer into your shipping just in case your shipping rates increase.

Shipping rates are determined by two factors—size and weight. You need to confine your boxes to the smallest and lightest container possible. Once you are done prototyping all your products, buy a few boxes of different sizes and shapes to see how you can fit your products in the least amount of space possible.

Make sure to take into account international shipping fees, too. Not all countries are created equal when it comes to international shipping, and you have to check each country's shipping rate individually because they vary wildly. I've seen rates range from ten to forty dollars for the same package, depending on the country you're shipping to. Forgetting about international shipping is a great way to go bankrupt.

Marketing – The fourth section of your budget is marketing. Marketing for your launch includes running ads, creating promotional materials, building websites, attending live events, filming videos, and anything you do to spread the word about your campaign. You can expect to spend up to 30 percent of your budget on marketing.

Marketing is a mandatory part of any campaign. Your goal is to get your product seen by the most people possible, which means doing a lot of promotion in the months leading up to your launch date, and especially during your campaign.

The problem with a marketing budget is that you have to invest in it whether your product is successful or not. Even if you pay yourself back after your launch is successful, you have to outlay the money for it up front. This is a scary scenario for most people, but it's also a necessary part of any successful launch.

If you have to save up for a successful marketing blitz, do it. Marketing is the difference between a mediocre campaign and a great one. That being said, don't spend money on marketing just to spend it. Do your research and pour your resources into the channels that give the best return.

Fees – The fifth section of your budget involves processing fees. No matter the outlet, fees are an inevitable part of your launch. Kickstarter and Indiegogo take 5–10 percent in fees when all is said and done, but even if you go with your own site, there will be fees associated with your credit card transactions.

Credit card processing fees can be as low as 2 percent and as high as 5 percent, depending on your processor and type of card the customer uses. You need to build those fees into your budget or you'll have a cash shortfall.

Additionally, most companies and sites that help produce or distribute your product will have setup fees associated with them. We've talked about many of them earlier—and I recommend adding those fees to their appropriate budget section—but if you don't want to do that, this is the catch-all section for all miscellaneous fees associated with your campaign.

Your time – The sixth section of the budget accounts for your time. Most creators think that paying themselves for their work during a campaign is gross. I disagree.

Working on a campaign is a massive amount of work and if you do it all for free—or, gods forbid, you lose money—it will be a miserable experience and you'll never want to do it again. I'm not saying you need to make a windfall, but at least factor in enough money to buy a bottle of champagne and take yourself out to a nice dinner.

Contingency – My favorite line item is the 10 percent contingency, because it's easy to calculate. After you have added everything else in your budget, add a 10 percent padding to the bottom line to account for anything that goes wrong with your campaign. There is always something that goes horribly wrong, and it's critical to have some extra money to deal with it.

You must take the time to properly construct your budget; it takes at least a month to prepare a budget appropriately. Most of it relies on other vendors getting back to you, but it's up to you to find those vendors, choose the right one for your project, and plug in all the numbers so you get a complete picture of your campaign goals.

The budget is the bedrock of your entire campaign. If you get it wrong, everything will collapse in on itself. If you can get it right, though, you'll have a solid foundation for success.

EVERY PRODUCT LAUNCH

IS FILLED WITH FEAR

I know you have a lump in your throat when thinking about launching your product. I wish I could tell you it goes away over time, but I can't. The truth is, I have it, too. Product launches are scary. Every launch I've ever had is filled with fear.

You will never have a perfect product launch. No matter what you do, there will always be problems. You will look back after each launch and notice fifty things you should have done differently. No matter how much you learn, there is always something to learn from the next one.

I launched my first campaign with a stable job and money coming in every month. I just needed my product launches to cover printing costs. That's not the case anymore.

Now, my launches have to pay my mortgage months into the future. They have to pay for teams of artists and designers. They have to pay for entire productions. Meanwhile, I still have to pay my bills. That's a scary proposition.

Even though I know how to launch products really well, there is always uncertainty. There will always be uncertainty. That's where the fear comes in for me, and it never goes away.

But you can tame that fear.

If you build the fundamental toolkit we've talked about throughout this book, the fear won't overwhelm you. It will always be there, but it will be muted. You will be able to overcome it.

It doesn't go away, but preparation makes it bearable.

At the end of the day, every new launch is stepping foot into the unknown. You are putting yourself out there and hoping people want what you have to offer.

Even thinking about launching a product right now gives me knots in the pit of my stomach, but it doesn't stop me. It invigorates me, because I know there is an audience for my products. I know that even if something isn't perfectly launched, I can make it work.

All of that confidence comes from launching products over and over again. It comes from getting knocked down and standing back up. It comes from success after success, and overcoming failure upon failure.

It comes from being in the game and staying in it.

If fear has been holding you back, I urge you to launch something as soon as possible. It doesn't have to be big. It doesn't have to be groundbreaking. It just has to be something so you can start developing your confidence for the future.

AFTERWORD

It's over!

If you've read this far, I want to thank you for your persistence and perseverance. I know that learning about business isn't any creator's favorite thing to do in the world; however, just by reading this book, you are so much further ahead than most creatives on this planet.

I would say to give yourself a round of applause, but I've worked very hard throughout this book not to be cheesy and don't want to ruin it now.

Well, maybe just a little applause would be okay. Not too long, though, because now the real work begins.

That's right…work.

As much knowledge as I crammed into this book, it's truly just a primer to gear you up for a lifelong pursuit of learning about the business of art. The goal of this book is to give you the necessary tools so you can go out there and build the foundation of a creative career.

It's not an endpoint. It's a beginning.

You made it to the end of this book. Now, you are prepared for the horrible and yet consistent world of late-stage capitalism. However, you still have to live in it.

If you loved this book, I hope you go check out *The Author Stack,* my weekly newsletter that goes into even more depth about how to build your creator career.

https://www.theauthorstack.com/

Find more of my work at my blog:

www.theauthorstack.com

Find all my work at my website:

www.russellnohelty.com

Bookbub:

https://www.bookbub.com/profile/russell-nohelty

www.ingramcontent.com/pod-product-compliance
Lightning Source LLC
Chambersburg PA
CBHW071554210326
41597CB00019B/3246